your guide to the law in Scotland

YCPS2

YOUNG CITIZEN'S PASSPORT SCOTLAND
second edition

INDIVIDUALS ENGAGING IN SOCIETY

 Citizenship Foundation

in association with
the Law Society
of Scotland

young citizen's passport
scotland

your guide to the **law** in scotland

The law affects all of our lives in one way or another. In spite of this, it is often difficult to be sure of exactly how different laws apply to us as individuals. The Law Society of Scotland believes it is important that all citizens have an awareness of their rights and responsibilities under the law. Our support of this booklet is one element of an outreach programme to promote awareness of these issues and to encourage discussion and debate about the law and legal issues amongst young citizens in Scotland.

I am delighted to have the opportunity of commending the Young Citizen's Passport Scotland to you. I am confident that you will find it a common sense and useful guide as you move on to meet the new challenges of work or further education.

Liz Campbell
Director (Education and Training)
The Law Society of Scotland

remember!

In trying to summarise the law, we have had to leave out some details that may be relevant to your own situation. So don't rely on this book as proof of your legal rights. Always take further advice before taking any legal action. Often the best place to start is the Citizens' Advice Bureau, but there are many others. Remember too that the law is always developing and changing. To the best of our knowledge we have described the law as it stood on 1st January 2007.

The law is often a blunt instrument and using it in the wrong way can make matters worse. Try to sort things out personally, if you can. It's generally better to use the legal system only as a last resort, when everything else has failed.

Hodder Gibson
www.hoddergibson.co.uk

YCP Scotland

The **YCP Scotland** has been produced by the **Citizenship Foundation**, an independent educational charity, which aims to empower individuals to engage in the wider community through education about the law, democracy and society. There are significant differences in certain sections of the law between Scotland and the rest of the UK, and we are grateful to the **Law Society of Scotland** for assistance in producing this Scottish edition of the Young Citizen's Passport.

The Citizenship Foundation,
63 Gee Street,
London EC1V 3RS

Tel 020 7566 4141
Fax 020 7566 4131

www.citizenshipfoundation.org.uk

Email
info@citizenshipfoundation.org.uk

Charity Reg. No. 801360

The Law Society of Scotland,
26 Drumsheugh Gardens,
Edinburgh EH3 7YR

Tel 0131 226 7411
Fax 0131 225 2934

www.lawscot.org.uk

Email lawscot@lawscot.org.uk

contents

05 life
19 safety
25 education
33 work & training
51 money
65 family
75 home
83 leisure
95 travel & transport
107 police & courts
119 law, government & human rights
133 european union
142 contacts

website information and guidance on scots law is available at www.lawscot.org.uk

INDIVIDUALS ENGAGING IN SOCIETY

Citizenship Foundation

The Citizenship Foundation would like to thank Hodder Gibson for their support in the production of this Scottish edition.

  As well as **The Law Society of Scotland**, we would like to thank the **Faculty of Advocates** for help and support in this project. For more information on Advocates, and their place in Scotland's legal system, please visit www.advocates.org.uk or contact Advocates Library, Parliament House, EDINBURGH EH11RF, tel 0131 226 5071.

Editor and main author Tony Thorpe.

Concept devised by Andrew Phillips OBE, President of the Citizenship Foundation.

We would like to thank Douglas Mill and Liz Campbell at The Law Society of Scotland; Sandy Wylie and Kirsty Hood at The Faculty of Advocates; lawyers at Maclay, Murray & Spens and at Anderson, Shaw and Gilbert; Hew Campbell (Royal Bank of Scotland); Mike Flynn (SSPCA); Paul Gilroy and James McKenna (Lothian and Borders Police); Tom Halbert and Eileen Taylor (Strathclyde Police); Michael McGrath (Scottish Catholic Education Service); Louise Adamson, Brian Allingham, Judith Chisholm, John Fotheringham, Janet Hood, Derek Livingston, Drew Livingstone, Dan Mace, John Mitchell, Sam Nicholson, Iain Nisbet (Govan Law Centre), Derek O'Carroll, Neil Ross, Richard Siddall and Neil Stevenson.

 Multiple copies from the first printing of this book have been sent to all secondary schools in Scotland via the distribution services of Learning Teaching Scotland, to whom thanks are offered for their assistance. The distribution was made possible by the generosity of the Law Society of Scotland as part of their outreach programme.

Designed and illustrated by Nomad Graphique; Mike Gibas, Lena Whitaker, Laura Emms, Mark Askam and Adam Williams.

Photographs AbleStock, PhotoDisc, PhotoAlto, Nomad Graphique, Ingram Publishing, Lenny Warren/Strathclyde Police, Scottish Executive and John Mitchell. Image of The Mace (page 119), and the Scottish Parliament building (cover and page 120) © Scottish Parliamentary Corporate Body

British Library Cataloguing in Publication Data
A catalogue record for this title is available from the British Library

ISBN-10: 0-340-92961-8
ISBN-13: 978-0-340-92961-2

Published by Hodder Gibson, 2a Christie Street, Paisley PA1 1NB.
Tel: 0141 848 1609; Fax: 0141 889 6315; Email: hoddergibson@hodder.co.uk

First published 2004
Second Edition 2007
Impression number   10   9   8   7   6   5   4   3   2   1
Year   2010 2009 2008 2007

Printed in Italy for Hodder Gibson, 2a Christie Street, Paisley, PA1 1NB, Scotland, UK.

life

06 health
09 drugs & the law
13 sex
15 pregnancy
17 hiv & aids

young citizen's **passport**

INDIVIDUALS
ENGAGING IN
SOCIETY

Citizenship Foundation

health

Doctors

Once you're 16, you can decide about your own health care – although, strictly speaking, doctors don't need to consult parents of patients who are under 16, as long as they believe the patient fully understands what is being proposed.

Confidentiality

Patients also have a right of confidentiality. Nothing they say to their doctor should be passed on to anyone else – not even the fact that they made an appointment.

General practitioners

Everyone living in the UK, including visitors from overseas, is entitled to register with a GP. A list of local doctors is available from your local NHS Board or NHS 24, main post office, library, tourist information office, and Citizens' Advice Bureau.

You have the right to change your GP at any time. You don't have to explain your reasons for doing so or tell the doctor concerned. However, a doctor does not have to accept you as a patient either. If you are refused in this way, the local NHS Board has a duty to give you details of local GPs. New patients are entitled to a health examination when they join a practice.

If you are staying for up to three months in another part of the United Kingdom, you can ask to be registered with another GP on a temporary basis. But if you are leaving home and going to college or university it's probably better to register with a new doctor in the town or city where you are staying, so you are guaranteed all the services of the practice if you ever need them. It's helpful to provide your medical card or National Health number when you register. If you don't have these, you will need to know your place of birth and the name and address of the doctor or practice with which you were previously registered.

PRESCRIPTIONS

Prescriptions are free if:
- **you are under 16;**
- **you are under 19 and in full-time education;**
- **you are pregnant or have had a baby in the last 12 months;**
- **you suffer from a serious illness;**
- **you or your partner receive Income Support, income-based Jobseeker's Allowance, Working Tax Credit or Child Tax Credit; or**
- **your name is on a current HC2 charges certificate.**

Further details are available from GPs, the Citizens' Advice Bureau and from libraries.

Anyone now claiming a free prescription will be asked to provide proof that they are entitled to do so. A person who cannot do this should not be refused the prescription, but a check on their entitlement may be made by a prescription fraud team.

use the law with care try talking first

Records Under the *Data Protection Act 1998*, you have a general right to see all your medical records – whether they are held on paper or on computer. You are also entitled to ask for a copy to take away. Access however may be refused if the doctor believes that seeing your records may cause you or someone else serious physical or mental harm.

Your GP or the hospital may ask you to pay for this service. The maximum charge to see your records (either on paper or on screen) is £10. The maximum charge for a copy of a computer-held record is also £10 – and £50 for records held manually.

If you believe that the information on your records is not correct, you may ask for it to be changed. The doctor, however, does not have to accept your opinion, but is required to note on your records what you have said.

DENTISTS

All British citizens are entitled to dental treatment provided by the National Health Service. However – unlike medical treatment from a GP – dental treatment is not always available free of charge.

NHS patients pay £15.50 for a check-up, £42.40 for treatment such as fillings or extractions, and up to a maximum of £189 (September 2006) for more complex work.

Dental treatment is free if:

- **you are under 18, or under 19 and still in full-time education; or**
- **you are pregnant or have had a baby within a year of starting treatment; or**
- **your name is on a current HC2 charges certificate; or**
- **you or your partner receive Income Support, income-based Jobseeker's Allowance, or have an NHS Tax Credit Exemption Certificate.**

Dentists can charge a patient who fails to keep an appointment or cancels at very short notice. The level of charge varies from one dentist to another.

Not all dentists provide NHS treatment. To find a list of NHS dentists in your area, look on the NHS website www.show.scot.nhs.uk, and search for 'dentist', call NHS 24 (see contacts) or look in the yellow pages, under dental surgeons. You don't have to be registered with a dentist to get NHS treatment; you can contact any surgery providing NHS treatment and ask if they have any NHS appointments available. However, it is usually much easier to obtain treatment if you have regular appointments with the same dentist.

Before each course of treatment, you will receive a treatment plan, showing the work the dentist intends to carry out and what it will cost. The dentist may offer to treat you privately, but should not place pressure on you by implying that the treatment is not available on the NHS. You do not have to accept the treatment being offered.

If you need emergency treatment and are not registered with a dentist, contact a local NHS dentist to see if they can take you on an emergency basis or get in touch with your local NHS Board. Many areas have dental access centres, providing NHS treatment and advice for emergency work and for those not registered for regular treatment. Details are available from your local NHS Board.

health

Opticians Eye tests are no longer free to everyone. You will get a free test if you:

- **are under 16 or under 19 and in full-time education;**
- **are partially sighted or need complex lenses;**
- **or your partner receive Income Support, income-based Jobseeker's Allowance, Working Tax Credit or Child Tax Credit; or**
- **your name is on a current HC2 Charges certificate.**

If you need glasses you may be entitled to help with buying them, particularly if you are unemployed or a student on a low income. Further information is available from opticians, the Citizens' Advice Bureau and booklet HC11, *Help with health costs*, available from libraries.

Complaints If you have a complaint about the NHS or your treatment, it's important to make it as soon as possible. Advice is available from NHS 24, tel 08454 24 24 24.

Tattoos It's illegal for a person to be given a tattoo if they are under 18.

The right to die The law states that a doctor may give a patient a painkilling drug, which shortens their life, as long as the intention is to relieve pain and suffering and not to kill. If the drug is given with the intention of ending that person's life, the doctor can face a charge of murder.

It is possible to make what is called a living will (known in law as an advance directive) setting out how you would like to be treated if you ever lose the capacity to make or convey a decision. You must clearly understand what you are doing when you give the directive and, although it is not legally binding on the doctor it' is an indication of your wishes and will be taken into consideration. An advance directive cannot authorise a doctor to do anything unlawful.

Wills Anyone aged 12 or over can make a will, provided they are capable of understanding what they are doing.

Blood There's no legal minimum age to become a blood donor, but the National Blood Service won't accept anyone under 17. Donors usually give about three quarters of a pint twice a year.

use the law with care **try talking first**

Controlled drugs

All drugs produce some kind of change in the way a person's body or mind works, and the availability of most drugs – whether aspirins, alcohol or amphetamines – is controlled by law.

The main law covering the use of dangerous drugs in Britain is the *Misuse of Drugs Act 1971*. Under this Act, drugs that people might misuse have been placed on a list of controlled drugs, and it is an offence to possess, produce or supply anyone with them. The list of controlled drugs is divided into three categories – Classes A, B and C. Penalties for possession and supply exist for all three classes, with Class A penalties the most severe.

CLASS A DRUGS

Cocaine is a white powder sometimes injected, but usually snorted, through a tube. Crack is cocaine treated with chemicals, so it can be smoked. Both give a high, followed by a rapid down. The only way to maintain the high is to keep taking the drug – but regular use leads to sickness, sleeplessness, weight loss, and addiction.

Heroin is made from the opium poppy – smoked, sniffed or injected. It comes as a white powder when pure. Street heroin is usually brownish white. Heroin slows down the brain and, at first, gives a feeling of total relaxation. Repeated use creates dependency. Overdosing causes unconsciousness and often death – particularly if used with other drugs, such as alcohol.

LSD, also known as acid, is a man-made substance, sold impregnated on blotting paper (often printed with cartoon characters or in colourful patterns) and dissolved on the tongue. It usually takes about an hour to work, and lasts up to 12 hours. The effects depend on the strength of the dose and the user's mood. It generally distorts feelings, vision and hearing, and bad trips lead to depression and panic, or worse, if the user is already anxious.

Ecstasy, or E, is sold as tablets of different shapes and colour. It makes the user feel friendly and full of energy, and sound and colours can seem much more intense. However, the comedown can leave the user tired and low – often for days. Regular users can have problems sleeping, and some women find it makes their periods heavier. Ecstasy affects the body's temperature control and it may cause the user to overheat and dehydrate. There is no guarantee that tablets sold as ecstasy do not contain some other ingredients. This can make their use unpredictable and dangerous.

Magic mushrooms grow in the wild and contain hallucinogens that, when eaten, have similar effects to LSD. Under the *Misuse of Drugs Act 1971* (as amended by the *Drugs Act 2005*) it is an offence to possess, sell or supply magic mushrooms. It is not illegal to pick or possess magic mushrooms in their raw state. However, it is illegal to prepare them in any way or to supply, or possess with the intention of supply, prepared mushrooms to another person. One of the most commonly used is the Liberty Cap. The effects of magic mushrooms are similar to a mild dose of LSD, with high blood pressure and possible stomach pains and vomiting. The greatest danger is in eating highly poisonous mushrooms, mistaking them for the hallucinogenic kind.

drugs and the law

CLASS B DRUGS

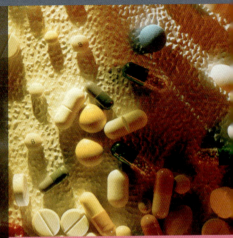

Amphetamines sold as pills or powder, were developed to treat depression. They give a feeling of energy and confidence, but increasing doses are needed to keep up the effect. The downside is anxiety, insomnia, irritability and less resistance to disease and, as with all illegal drugs, there is no guarantee that they do not contain other harmful substances.

Barbiturates are used in medicine to help people who cannot sleep. They produce feelings of drowsiness and relief from anxiety. Sold as a powder or coloured capsule. Regular use creates dependency. Extremely dangerous when taken with alcohol or other drugs.

CLASS C DRUGS

Tranquillisers cause lower alertness, and affect people who drive or operate machinery. A number of anabolic steroids are also on the list of controlled drugs after concern over their misuse in sport and bodybuilding.

Cannabis was reclassified from a Class B drug to a Class C in January 2004, but possession and supply of the drug remain illegal. In England and Wales, a person found using cannabis might or might not be arrested depending upon the circumstances and the person's age. In Scotland, possession of cannabis remains an arrestable offence. Scottish police procedures in relation to cannabis remain unchanged by reclassification, and anyone found in possession will be reported to the Procurator Fiscal, who will decide what further action to take.

Cannabis comes in a solid dark lump, known as resin, or as dried leaves, called grass. The effects vary from one person to another. Some feel relaxed and happy, but the downside can be moodiness, anxiety, and difficulties with memory. Heavy users risk great tiredness, mental heath problems, and cancer – from the chemical constituents.

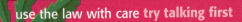

use the law with care **try talking first**

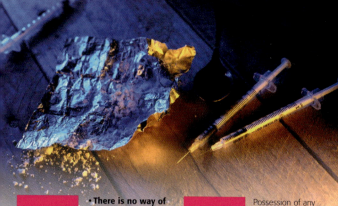

The risks

• There is no way of knowing exactly what is in drugs made or obtained illegally. This makes them unpredictable and dangerous.

- All drugs have side effects that may be dangerous and even fatal – particularly if they are mixed or taken regularly.
- Anyone using shared needles, filters, or spoons, risks becoming infected with hepatitis or HIV, the virus that leads to AIDS.
- Hepatitis C is a newly discovered virus that can cause severe long term liver damage. It is caused by blood to blood contact, generally through sharing needles when injecting drugs.
- Employers and head teachers have a legal duty to confiscate drugs found at work or school and hand them to the police as quickly as possible.
- Illegal drug-taking places a person's job, school, or college place at risk.
- A person prosecuted for illegal drug use will not necessarily be sent to prison, but could end up with a criminal record. However, a prison sentence is a strong possibility for someone found guilty of supply.

Possession

Possession of any controlled drug, even if it's only a tiny amount, is an arrestable offence. Those found in possession are reported to the Procurator Fiscal (see page 116), who will decide upon the next course of action.

Supply

It is an offence under the *Misuse of Drugs Act 1971* to supply or to offer to supply someone with a controlled drug. Obviously this includes the sale of drugs – but it is still an offence even if money does not change hands. Giving a controlled drug to a friend or sharing a drug at a party by passing it from one person to another is still seen in law as supply.

It is also an offence if the substance sold is not actually a controlled drug, but the seller claimed or believed it to be one.

Production

It is an offence under the *Misuse of Drugs Act 1971* to produce any controlled drug. This includes letting someone use your kitchen or a room for this purpose.

Growing cannabis comes under this heading, and is an offence if you knew what you were doing.

drugs and the law

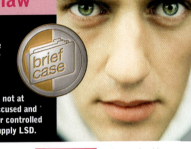

■ BRIEF CASE: Dennis

Dennis bought 1,000 tabs of what he thought was LSD, and was caught by the police trying to sell them. When the tablets were analysed they were found not to contain LSD, but a harmless vegetable product that was not at all illegal. Despite this, Dennis was accused and found guilty of supplying an illegal or controlled drug, because his intention was to supply LSD.

Police powers

If a police officer has reasonable grounds to suspect that someone is in possession of a controlled drug, the officer can search that person and their vehicle and seize anything that seems to be evidence of an offence.

Glue sniffing

The effect of solvent abuse is rather like getting drunk on alcohol. However, it takes effect more quickly as the substances enter the bloodstream through the lungs rather than the stomach. Sniffers may experience hallucinations and, if plastic bags are used, may become unconscious or choke on their own vomit. Glue sniffing itself is not against the law, but it is an offence to supply a solvent to anyone if there is reasonable cause to believe that the fumes might be inhaled. It is also an offence to sell lighter fuel to anyone under 18.

Tobacco

Tobacco should not be sold by law to anyone who seems to be under the age of 16. Under the *Children and Young Persons (Protection from Tobacco) Act 1991*, shopkeepers can be fined up to £2,500 for selling tobacco or cigarettes to under age children. Police officers and uniformed park keepers have, in law, powers to confiscate smoking materials from anyone under 16 smoking in a public place. The Scottish Executive plans to raise the age limit for tobacco sales to 18 by October 2007. As before, shopkeepers who sell tobacco to anyone who seems to be under the age of 18 may face heavy fines.

For details of the law and alcohol, see **leisure**, pages 84–85.

Information

Know The Score is a free Scottish Helpline providing information and advice on drugs 24 hours a day, on 0800 587 5879. Information is also available on the website **www.knowthescore.info**

■ BRIEF CASE: Alex

Alex was one of a group who bought and sold drugs for themselves and other students at their university. One day, his friend Paul took an overdose of heroin and died. It was Alex who had supplied the drug. A court sentenced him to five years in prison.

use the law with care try talking first

Not the whole story

Although sex is discussed much more now than it was in the past, most people at some stage in their lives get confused about what they should and should not be doing. Probably the best advice is:

- **don't believe everything you hear;**
- **decide what is right for you and your partner;**
- **talk to your partner and think about their point of view.**

You don't have to do anything that you are not comfortable with. Nor should you expect your partner to. There is no golden age by which you should have had sex. Some people will choose not to because they are not interested, or because there hasn't yet been the right opportunity, or because they want to wait until they are married. There's plenty of time and it's OK to opt out.

Pressurising someone into going further than they want, as well as being morally wrong, can reach a stage where it is also against the law. For example, even kissing or touching someone without their agreement can be an assault. In law, both people must agree to what they are doing (known as consent), and they must understand what is happening. The person who gets someone drunk in order to go to bed with them, or takes advantage of their drunken state, risks being charged with rape. (See **safety**, page 23).

Sex and girls

Age of consent

A girl must be 16 before she can legally have sex with a boy. If she has sex before this, her male partner is breaking the law. Girls, unlike boys, cannot be prosecuted for having sex under the age of 16.

The law doesn't usually get involved in punishing girls or women for having sex, although a woman who has sex with a boy under 16 may be prosecuted for 'shameless indecency' or 'lewd and indecent practices', even if he consents.

Sex and boys

Unlawful sex

It is an offence for a boy or a man to have sex with a girl under 16 – even if she agrees.

If the girl is under 13, the maximum penalty is life imprisonment, since a girl of 12 or under is assumed by the law not to understand the consequences of having sex. A man who has sex with a girl aged 13–15 can be given a prison sentence of up to ten years. A man aged 24 or over has no defence and will be found guilty. If he is under 24, has never been charged with the same offence, and can show he genuinely believed the girl was 16 or over, he may be found not guilty.

A boy aged eight or over can be prosecuted for having sex with a girl who is under 13, and it's no defence for the boy to say in court that the girl agreed.

Lesbian and gay relationships

For women

Lesbian relationships are lawful. The law says nothing about lesbianism in general.

For men

Gay relationships are lawful if both men consent, are 16 or over, and act in private.

For all

There can be difficulties for lesbian and gay people when some people have a different moral view of homosexual relationships.

If you need to talk to someone who understands, see **contacts** for groups who may be able to help.

Contraception

Each person who has sex is responsible for guarding against the risks to both people. It is important to know how to use contraceptives properly and how they affect your body. Good advice is therefore vital. For this you can go to a family planning clinic, your doctor or a Brook Advisory Centre. If you're under 16, a doctor can prescribe contraceptives for you without telling your parents – as long as the doctor believes that you are mature enough to understand what is being proposed. Condoms can easily be bought from supermarkets, garages, chemists, from slot machines in toilets and by mail order. Femidoms, which are a form of sheath for women, are sold in chemists. Both these and condoms are available free from family planning clinics.

The British Pregnancy Advisory Service now prescribes the morning after pill in advance of need, see **contacts**.

Emergency

If you have had sex without using contraception – or used a condom that split – emergency contraception is available to stop you becoming pregnant.

This form of contraception is for emergencies only. It is not as reliable as the Pill or condoms, and does not protect against sexual diseases. Some people also believe it represents a form of early abortion.

The emergency contraceptive pill is available free from your GP or a family planning clinic, and should be taken within 72 hours of unprotected sex. It can also be bought from most chemists – but some do not sell it to girls under 16.

An IUD, which may also be used to prevent a pregnancy must be fitted by a trained doctor.

use the law with care try talking first

You think you're pregnant

Your period is late and you think you might be pregnant. What do you do? To find out if you are expecting a baby, you can:

- **see your doctor;**
- **speak to someone you trust – partner, family member, friend,**
- **buy a pregnancy testing kit from a chemist. These are generally accurate and cost between £6–£10;**
- **visit a family planning clinic or a Brook Advisory Centre, who will offer confidential advice and provide a free test with an immediate result.**

What if it's positive?

You will have three choices: to go through with the pregnancy and bring up your child; to give the baby over to be adopted; or to have an abortion and terminate the pregnancy.

None of these may be wholly right – just the best in the circumstances. It is vital that you do everything possible to make the right decision for much hangs upon it, and the consequences can last two lifetimes. So talk, if you can, to your partner in the pregnancy, your parents, good friends, and your doctor.

Adoption

Giving up a baby for adoption is not easy – for the mother or father. It's best to talk to someone about this, such as your doctor or someone at the antenatal clinic, as soon as possible.

The adoption will probably be handled by a social worker who will discuss the kind of family the birth parents want their child to grow up in and will try to find out as much as possible about the birth family to pass on to the adopters.

Adopters usually have to be married, but the *Adoption and Children (Scotland) Act 2006*, which was passed by the Scottish Parliament on 8 December 2006, will allow unmarried couples (including same sex couples) to adopt if they can provide a suitable home.

When the child has settled down with the new family, the adoptive parents can apply to the adoption centre at the local Sheriff court for an adoption order, which will be granted if the court is satisfied that all is well.

Neither birth parent has the right to see their child after she or he has been adopted, although the court can give permission for contact and the child can get in touch with them after they are 18. Help and advice for anyone thinking of having their child adopted is available through the British Agencies for Adoption and Fostering, see **contacts**.

ABORTION

The question of whether a person should have an abortion has serious moral and practical consequences. Those who are totally opposed to abortion believe that the unborn baby has a right to life in all (or almost all) circumstances. For others, however, it is the situation and feelings of the mother that should determine the best course of action. For anyone thinking of having an abortion it is almost always helpful to talk to someone about it. This can be a doctor, staff at the local family planning clinic or one of the other organisations listed in contacts.

Abortion in Scotland is legal as long as it follows the law set out in the *Abortion Act 1967.*

This states that an abortion may be legally carried out if two doctors agree that:

- continuing the pregnancy would risk the life of the mother; or
- the mother is less than 24 weeks pregnant and continuation would risk injury to her physical or mental health or that of her other children; or
- there is a substantial risk that the child will be born severely handicapped.

Concern over the mother's mental health is a common reason for doctors to allow an abortion – particularly if they feel she is likely to suffer excessive emotional strain.

An abortion must by law, except in a few extreme cases, be carried out before the twenty fourth week of pregnancy. Anyone wanting to have an abortion using the National Health Service will need to start making the arrangements before the twelfth week.

If you are under 16, your parents must give their consent to end the pregnancy, unless two doctors decide that you are mature enough to understand what the decision really means. Doctors normally insist on having a parent's consent before giving a young person a general anaesthetic. An abortion can take place without anaesthetic, through tablets. But these are normally used only within the first eight weeks of a pregnancy.

The father, whether he is married to the mother or not, has no right to prevent her from having a legal abortion.

A doctor does not have to carry out an abortion if it is against his or her conscience. If this happens, you can arrange to see another doctor.

use the law with care **try talking first**

What is HIV?

To understand HIV – standing for human immunodeficiency virus – you have to know something about the immune system that stops us from getting ill.

Blood plays an important part in our body's defence against illness. It contains millions of cells, about one per cent of which are white. A particularly important type of white cell is called the t-helper cell, and one of the jobs of these cells is to fight off infection.

HIV is a virus that attacks the t-helper cells. If it grows inside these cells, and other germs get into our body, we have no way of fighting infection. We become ill and develop what is called acquired immune deficiency syndrome, known as AIDS.

HIV is the cause of AIDS, although not everyone who is HIV positive goes on to suffer the effects associated with the syndrome.

How do you get HIV?

The HIV virus is found in the blood, semen, or vaginal fluid of a person with HIV or AIDS. Infection takes place when these fluids pass from an infected person into the bloodstream of someone else. This can happen in several ways:

- **by having unprotected sex with someone who already has the HIV virus. This means putting a penis into a vagina or anus without using a condom. The risk of contracting HIV infection through unprotected oral sex is thought to be much lower – but transmission is possible if semen, vaginal fluid, or menstrual blood come into contact with bleeding gums or mouth infections. You can help to protect yourself from HIV infection through sex by using a condom;**
- **by using or sharing a hypodermic needle, which has already been used by someone with HIV, leading to the exchange of a small amount of infected blood;**
- **as a result of a mother with HIV passing it on to her baby whilst it is growing inside her.**

Blood transfusions in industrialised countries should be safe as the blood used is routinely screened.

Anyone who feels they may be at risk of HIV or AIDS should seek medical advice and help, see **contacts**.

How don't you get HIV?

The HIV virus dies quickly once outside the body. Because of this, you don't get HIV from:
• hugging • kissing, including French kisses • sharing towels or cutlery • swimming • toilet seats • sharing musical instruments • giving blood.

HIV and the law

If you know that you are HIV positive, it is a serious offence to have unprotected sex with a partner without telling them you are infected.

hiv and aids

Sexually transmitted infections (also called venereal disease, VD or the clap) are caught from sexual contact with people who have the infection themselves. Most STIs can be cured if treated as soon as possible, and so if you have had sex and you have sores or pain around your sexual organs, see a doctor straightaway. Don't have sex with anyone until it's cleared up, because you will put your partner's health at risk too.

However, not all STIs show signs of infection. Anyone who has sex with someone who is not their regular partner is at risk, particularly if they fail to use a condom. Chlamydia, for example, can pass undetected for some time, but may eventually produce pain and discomfort, and cause infertility in men and give women problems in conceiving.

Advice and treatment on sexually transmitted infections is available from clinics dealing with family planning, pregnancy or genito-urinary medicine, as well as family doctors. It is entirely confidential, although if you are under 16, the doctor may be reluctant to do anything without consulting your parents. If this is the case, it is worth checking first.

HIV and work

If you have HIV or AIDS, you are under no obligation to tell your employer. However, the government advises any health care worker who believes themself to be at risk from infection to seek medical advice immediately. Your employer has a legal duty to treat the information that you are HIV positive as confidential. As a rule, employers are not entitled to tell other workers that an employee is infected with HIV, without his or her permission.

Employers may, if they wish, ask all those who apply for a job to take an HIV test. However, if they do, this information must not be used to discriminate against anyone. Since October 2004, it has been against the law, under the *Disability Discrimination Act*, for employers to discriminate against someone with HIV/AIDS. This applies to all organisations, except the armed forces.

If you are worried about HIV or AIDS, support and help is available, see **contacts**.

Prostitution

Prostitutes sell sex for money. They can be either men or women. It is an offence for a prostitute to attract "business" in public (called importuning or soliciting) and for a man to try to obtain the services of a prostitute from a motor vehicle that he is in, or has just got out of. Prostitutes also risk physical abuse, sexually transmitted diseases, HIV or AIDS and pregnancy.

If the police become aware that a young person under the age of 16 is involved in prostitution, they will almost certainly inform social services who will decide whether to apply for an order to take that person into care.

safety

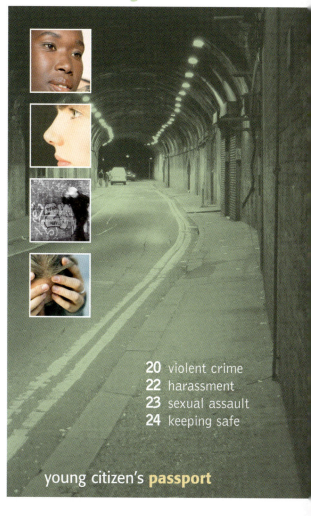

20 violent crime
22 harassment
23 sexual assault
24 keeping safe

young citizen's **passport**

INDIVIDUALS ENGAGING IN SOCIETY

Citizenship Foundation

violent crime

Fighting back

If you're threatened or hit, it's usually better to try to avoid a fight by talking to your attacker or backing off calmly.

If you can't do this, the law says that you can use reasonable force to defend yourself. This means that you're entitled to fight back, but not to go over the top and beat up the other person. If you do, you will have also committed an offence.

There is no law which says that you must report a crime to the police. If you want to claim compensation for your injuries, the crime must first have been reported to the police.

Arrest – doing it yourself

If you see someone committing a serious offence or have reasonable grounds for believing that they have committed one, you can make a citizen's arrest. But, take care. People have been hurt and even killed trying to do their civic duty. The best advice is to take in as much as you can about the incident, and then to ring the police. If you do get involved, remember that an ordinary person only has the power to make an arrest for a serious offence – such as theft, serious assault, or burglary. Don't arrest someone for parking on a double yellow line.

Neighbourhood patrols also come up against this problem. They can't arrest someone who they think is about to commit an offence (it must already have been done), nor can they use excessive force – otherwise they can face charges of assault and wrongful arrest.

Victims of violent crime

Victims of violent crime can apply to the *Criminal Injuries Compensation Authority* for compensation for their injuries – which must be serious enough to receive an award. The crime must be reported to the police without delay, and an application for compensation made within two years of the incident that caused the injury. However, all cases are treated individually and an exception can be made if, for example, the delay in reporting was caused by the after effects of the crime.

Victim Support runs a helpline and gives advice to victims of crime. Their number is in the local phone book, see **contacts**.

If you are a victim of crime and called as a witness, you can arrange to see a courtroom before the case starts, have a seat reserved for someone accompanying you, and ask to wait separately from other people. Details are available from the Scottish Court Service, see **contacts**.

■ BRIEF CASE: Raj

Raj ran an off-licence, and had twice been the victim of armed robbery. One night, a man carrying a long knife came into the shop demanding money from the till. As Raj was being held with a knife to his throat, his brother came through from the back and the robber ran off. Raj was so angry that he got into his van and chased the man down the street knocking him down and killing him. Raj was found guilty of manslaughter and sentenced to two and a half years imprisonment. The Court decided that he could not have been acting in self-defence because he was, by that time, not being attacked or threatened.

use the law with care **try talking first**

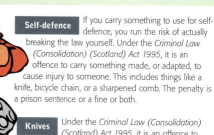

Self-defence If you carry something to use for self-defence, you run the risk of actually breaking the law yourself. Under the *Criminal Law (Consolidation) (Scotland) Act 1995*, it is an offence to carry something made, or adapted, to cause injury to someone. This includes things like a knife, bicycle chain, or a sharpened comb. The penalty is a prison sentence or a fine or both.

Knives Under the *Criminal Law (Consolidation) (Scotland) Act 1995*, it is an offence to have anything with a blade or sharp point in a public place. Folded pocket knives are allowed as long as the blade is less than 3" long. Schools are specifically mentioned as places where articles with blades or points must not be carried, and the police have the power to enter and search school premises if they have a good reason to believe that an offence of this kind has been committed. The penalty is a prison sentence or a fine.

SOME WORDS THEY USE

Assault Assault in law is an attack on a person whether this is by the act of actually hitting that person or using force (even very little force). Assault also takes place when a person causes someone to fear that they are about to suffer immediate unlawful physical violence for example by the use of threatening words.

In Scotland there is no distinction as in England and Wales between various types of assault, though there is an offence of aggravated assault where a weapon is used.

Theft by housebreaking Theft by housebreaking, despite the name, takes place when a person enters any building without permission intending to steal. Even if nothing is taken or done, a crime has still been committed. It's enough in law to prove that the person intended to break the law in this way.

Robbery Stealing something with the use or threat of force.

Theft There are, in law, three parts to theft. A person is guilty of theft who
(i) dishonestly takes something, which
(ii) belongs to someone else, and
(iii) intends to deprive that person of it permanently.

harassment

Abusive behaviour   It is an offence to use threatening, abusive or insulting words or behaviour in public in a way that is intended to cause a person harassment, alarm, or distress. It's also an offence to put up a sign or a poster that is threatening or abusive in the same way.

This kind of conduct in Scotland is likely to amount to the offence of breach of the peace. Under the *Criminal Law (Consolidation) (Scotland) Act 1995* there is also the separate offence of racially-aggravated harassment and it is also an offence to harass someone on the basis of their religion.

The law is designed to protect anyone who is being treated like this because, for example, of their race, disability, religion or sexuality. Harassment of this kind is a crime – just like any other – and can be reported to the police, who have a duty to investigate and to try to find those responsible. Statements from witnesses will strengthen a case.

Punishment for offences that can be shown to be racially or religiously aggravated, such as harassment, assault and criminal damage carry increased penalties.

Local councils also have a number of powers they can use to help tenants or homeowners in their area who are being racially harassed or attacked. They can prosecute residents for harassing or causing nuisance to other residents, they can get a court order stopping people committing certain types of anti-social behaviour, or, if those responsible are council tenants, they can evict them from their home.

The police or local authority can also apply for an anti-social behaviour order.

Stalking   There is no specific offence in Scotland directed to cover stalking behaviour but

■ BRIEF CASE: Marcia

Marcia and her 10 year old son were not the only black people on their estate, but for some reason faced almost continuous trouble from one particular group of boys. Marcia first tried ignoring the problem and then spoke to the boys and tried to talk to their parents. Nothing worked. Eventually she complained to the council who investigated the case and obtained a court order requiring the parents of one of the boys to leave their house, which they rented from the council. The boy's parents appealed, saying it was not their offensive behaviour but that of their son. The appeal was dismissed. The judge said that Marcia and her son should not be deprived of their rights just because the parents could not control their son.

it is likely to amount to the offence of breach of the peace. This offence covers conduct which may reasonably be expected to cause any person to be alarmed, upset or annoyed or to provoke a disturbance of the peace.

Someone who feels they might be a victim of harassment can apply to a court, for what is known as an interdict, ordering the person committing the offence to keep a certain distance from the victim's house or place of work. The victim can also apply for compensation for the worry they have suffered or for loss of earnings through time off work.

use the law with care try talking first

What if it happens to me? It all depends on the situation. If it's an isolated incident and the person is someone you don't know, then it may be best to try and ignore it. If you react and get abusive yourself, you run the risk of finding yourself in a far worse situation.

However, if it's happened before, or you're being harassed where you live, then it's important to tell the police – for your own safety. If you are getting abuse at school, college or at work, try and sort it out with the people concerned, but if that's not possible, or successful, raise it with someone in authority, who will have a legal duty to help you. See also the section on **discrimination** (page 44).

Someone suffering serious abuse or harassment may be able to claim compensation from the Criminal Injuries Compensation Authority (see page 20 and **contacts**).

sexual assault

Indecent assault It is an offence to touch or threaten a person in an indecent way. Groping and unwanted fondling can come into this category. Indecent assault carries a punishment of up to life imprisonment.

Rape If a male, aged eight or over, has vaginal intercourse with a female, and either that person doesn't want him to or he doesn't care if she is consenting, then the male has committed the crime of rape. It's also an offence to force someone to have sex against their will, or to give them drugs in the hope that they will give in.

Under Scottish law, rape can only be committed by a man on a woman. A similar assault by a man on another is not at the moment classed as rape, although it is still a criminal offence. This matter is now being considered by the Scottish Law Commission, which is reviewing the law relating to rape and other sexual offences in Scotland and may recommend changes to the law when it reports to Ministers in 2007.

Going out with someone is not, in law, an invitation to have sexual intercourse with them. Forcing another person to have sex is rape, and it's no defence for the man to say that he was drunk.

It's also rape if the victim had too much alcohol or other drugs to know what they were doing.

A wife doesn't have to have sex with her husband. If she does not consent, it's rape.

If you are raped Although you may not want to tell anyone, most police stations now have women officers who have been trained to deal with victims of sexual offences in a sensitive way.

If you are a woman, you can ask to be examined by a female doctor and you can take along your parents or a friend.

sexual assault

The police will be able to gather evidence more easily if you report the rape or assault as soon as possible. Reporting the crime early also makes your evidence more believable in court.

Once a victim tells the police that they have been raped or sexually assaulted, or the suspect has been charged, the victim has the right in law to remain anonymous. The victim cannot be questioned in court by the accused (although she can be questioned by the accused's lawyers), nor can their name and address or picture be reported in the media. Attempted rape is dealt with in the same way.

Help is available from *Victim Support* and the local *Rape Crisis Centre*, who will talk to any girl or woman who has suffered an unpleasant sexual experience. *Survivors UK* offer an advice service for men, see **contacts**. Victims of rape can apply for compensation to the *Criminal Injuries Compensation Authority*, see **contacts**.

Male victims of serious sexual assaults are treated in the same way as female victims.

Accused of rape If you are accused of raping someone, immediately contact a solicitor. Rape is a serious crime, and the punishment can be severe.

keeping safe

There are some simple steps that both men and women can take to make themselves safer.

- **If you go out – especially at night – tell someone where you are going. If possible, stay away from known danger spots.**
- **Keep your drink within your sights at all times.**
- **If you're out late, get a lift back if you can with someone you trust, or book a taxi, see page 88.**
- **If you walk home, try to get someone to go with you.**
- **Don't have expensive possessions like mobile phones on show.**
- **Check on the security of your home. Ordinary bolts and chains are not expensive.**
- **Knowing some self-defence can give you a feeling of greater confidence.**
- **If you carry a screech alarm keep it ready in your hand, not in your pocket or handbag.**
- **Men can help by taking care not to frighten women. For example, if you're walking in the same direction as a woman at night, don't walk behind her, cross over the road and walk on the other side.**
- **If you are facing some kind of harassment, tell someone about it. Ignoring it can make you more vulnerable.**

Abusive telephone calls It is an offence under the *Communications Act 2003* to make malicious and threatening phone calls, or to send such text messages.

If you get such a call, try not to react and don't start talking to the caller. Don't hang up, but put the receiver down and walk away for a few minutes. Try to do something else, and then put the handset back without checking if the caller is still there. If the phone rings again, pick up the receiver and don't say anything – a genuine caller will speak first. Advice on dealing with calls of this kind is available from BT, tel (free) 0800 666 700.

education

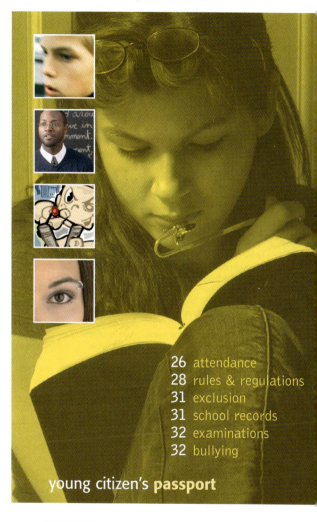

26 attendance
28 rules & regulations
31 exclusion
31 school records
32 examinations
32 bullying

young citizen's **passport**

INDIVIDUALS
ENGAGING IN
SOCIETY

Citizenship Foundation

attendance

The rights of children

A child is defined as someone who is not over school age. It is however presumed that a child of twelve years or more is old enough and mature enough to form a view of their own. Parents should take their child's views into consideration when any major decision is being made that affects them. Schools and teachers also have to consider pupils' views when taking decisions that will significantly affect them.

Which school?

Education authorities normally offer school places to children on the basis of designated catchment areas. Parents (but not children) have, however, the right to request a place at a school outwith the catchment area. Education authorities have a duty to meet such requests, unless there is a ground for refusal (e.g. the school is full). In most areas of Scotland, education authorities offer the choice of denominational (mostly Catholic) schools which are open to all.

If admission to a particular school is refused, parents (but not children) have a right to appeal against the decision and should be told how to go about this in the letter of refusal.

Further information may be obtained from the publication "Choosing a School" or from the Parentzone Website, see **contacts**.

Parents who cannot agree between themselves on a choice of school can ask a court to decide where their child will be educated. In this situation, the court must listen to and respect the wishes of the child concerned.

Attendance

Parents have the main responsibility, in law, for their child's education. Under the law it is the duty of parents of children of school age, to 'provide efficient education … suitable to his age, ability and aptitude either by causing him to attend a public school regularly or by other means'. The words 'by other means' are important here because it allows parents to educate their children in an independent school or out of school (e.g. at home). If a child is already in school, their parents must get permission from the local authority before withdrawing them from school. Permission should only be refused if there is good reason for concern.

Costs

State education is free and it is unlawful for schools to try to make parents pay for books or equipment that pupils need for subjects or activities taken in school hours as part of the school curriculum.

use the law with care try talking first

However, charges may be made for:

- **materials for practical subjects (if the pupil wants to keep the finished product);**
- **optional trips taken outside school hours;**
- **board and lodging on school trips, even if the activity is part of the school timetable.**

The education authority has a duty to provide pupils with free school transport or passes if their school is not within "walking distance", (three miles in most cases, two miles if the child is under eight years of age), where the route home is unsuitable to walk on, or it means crossing a dangerous road. This does not apply when the pupil has been offered a place in their local catchment area school, but attends a different school because of a placing request..

Local authorities may, in certain circumstances, also offer grants to assist with clothing.

An Education Maintenance Allowance scheme for 16 to 19 year olds is available to young people from low income families who are attending a full-time course at school or college.

Pupils at school, are entitled to free school meals if their parents (or they themselves) receive Income Support or income-based Jobseeker's Allowance, some types of Tax Credits or support under the *Immigration and Asylum Act 1999*. Pupils who bring a packed lunch must be provided with somewhere appropriate to eat it.

a slightly younger or older age, as all children begin on the same date (in August). A child is assumed to be of school age on the first school start date following their fifth birthday. However, parents of children who might exceptionally begin school before their fifth birthday (e.g. if they are born in September) may delay their child's school start date until the following August.

Compulsory education ends at the age of sixteen. By law, young people whose sixteenth birthday falls between 1st March and 30th September may leave school on 31st May of that year. Young people whose birthday falls between 1st October and the last day of February the following year may leave school at the beginning of their school's Christmas holidays.

Parents of a young person who has passed compulsory school age cannot force them to stay on at school against their wishes.

Leaving school or staying on

Children generally begin primary school at age five. Depending on when someone's birthday falls, they may begin school at

attendance

Truancy

Parents have a legal duty to make sure that their children attend school regularly or are suitably educated elsewhere. If they fail to do this, they may be committing a criminal offence and may be prosecuted. If a child is not attending school regularly, they may be referred to the children's panel for a hearing. The children's panel includes people from across the community. The panel can decide on measures to be taken such as supervision requirements or even removing the child from the home, depending on the reason for the hearing.

rules & regulations

Religious worship and education

The law states that all pupils in Scotland (including those between 16 and 18) should receive religious education and take part in religious observance, for example in assembly. Parents may withdraw their children from these, but this must not interfere with the attendance of the pupil at school. Pupils cannot opt out of religious education or worship themselves; it must be done by their parents.

Sex education

The law states that all secondary schools must provide sex education for their pupils and in a way that recognises the moral issues involved. However, a parent can request that their child be excluded from receiving sex education and the school must follow this request.

Schools can also discuss questions of sexual orientation with pupils as long as it is done in a way that 'has due regard to moral considerations and the values of family life'. Pupils must also learn about the nature of marriage and its importance for family life and the bringing up of children.

Government guidelines encourage teachers to involve parents and other appropriate professionals if they are asked for help by a pupil with a sexual or relationship problem.

Punishment

Teachers are entitled to impose punishments – but these must be reasonable. This allows a school to keep a pupil in detention during school hours. If a school wants to keep a child in after school they should get the parent's agreement first. Also, the detention must be reasonable in the circumstances and necessary for disciplinary reasons.

Pupils should not be held in detention for too long, nor should their safety be put at risk, e.g. if, as a consequence, they miss the last bus home.

School uniform

In 2001 the Scottish Executive produced a report called *Better Behaviour – Better Learning* which recommended that every school should agree a dress code with parents and pupils. Once this has been agreed it becomes a school rule and disciplinary sanctions may be imposed if pupils do not wear the uniform.

Grants may be available to assist with the purchase of school uniforms.

Confiscation

Teachers may confiscate any forbidden items, such as mobile phones, jewellery etc., which they should keep safe and return to the pupil after a reasonable time.

If illegal drugs or weapons are found, teachers must confiscate the items and hand them over to the police.

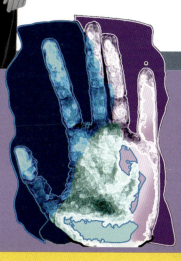

CORPORAL PUNISHMENT

Corporal punishment is banned in all schools in Scotland – although there are circumstances, under the law, when a member of staff may require to use reasonable force to prevent a pupil from injuring themselves or someone else or damaging property.

However, if a teacher uses excessive force, he or she may have committed an assault, which can give rise to both criminal charges and a civil claim for damages.

rules & regulations

DRUGS IN SCHOOL

Schools are encouraged to make clear what action they will take if pupils are found to be using, possessing or supplying illegal drugs in school.

Pupils can be excluded from school temporarily or permanently, but this should not be automatic, even though using or possessing drugs is a criminal offence. Schools should deal with cases individually and take into account the circumstances surrounding each incident. Although in most cases it will be important to tell parents of their child's involvement with illegal drugs, schools are not legally required to do so.

Schools do not have to act on rumours that a pupil is taking drugs in or out of school, but head teachers would ordinarily inform the police when illegal drugs are found on a pupil or on school premises. A teacher cannot always guarantee confidentiality for a pupil who might privately explain that he or she is taking drugs. The law allows a teacher to search a student's locker or desk, if it is suspected that it contains illegal drugs (or any other unlawful items). A pupil who is believed to be in possession of illegal drugs can be asked to empty their pockets. If they refuse, the police should be called to deal with the situation. A teacher should never carry out an intimate search.

If a head teacher decides to call the police, efforts must be made to contact the pupil's parents. A young person under 16 should not be interviewed by the police without a parent, adult friend or social worker being present.

use the law with care **try talking first**

without considering the individual circumstances of the case. A temporary exclusion is usually for a set length of time lasting from a half day to several weeks.

When pupils are excluded from school, their parents must be told without delay, and should receive a letter explaining the reasons for the exclusion, how long it will last or if it's permanent, and how they can appeal against it.

Parents, young people and children with legal capacity (usually, age 12 or over) have a right of appeal against an exclusion. The appeal is heard by an education appeal committee. There is a further right of appeal to the sheriff court.

When a pupil is excluded from school, the school (or education authority) should provide them with alternative education instead (e.g. sending work home, home tuition, allocating a new school etc.).

Further details may be obtained from the Parentzone Website at www.parentzonescotland.gov.uk, see **contacts**.

A pupil may be excluded from school if either:

- **their parent(s) are breaking school rules or disciplinary requirements or encouraging or allowing the pupil to do so; or**
- **allowing the pupil to remain at school would be seriously detrimental to order and discipline at the school or the educational wellbeing of the pupils there.**

Guidance from the Scottish Executive says that exclusion should only be used as a last resort. A pupil who breaks the law should not automatically be excluded

school records

Under the *Data Protection Act 1998*, pupils of any age have the right to see their school records. They need to put their request in writing, and the request should only be turned down if the pupil does not understand what he or she is asking for.

Parents also have the right to see their child's records, at least until he or she reaches 16. However the school can withhold certain items if it feels they might damage the mental or physical health of the pupil or someone else. Some sensitive personal information might not be disclosed to parents on the grounds of confidentiality for the pupil.

examinations

The vast majority of Scottish pupils sit exams administered by the SQA (Scottish Qualifications Authority). If a pupil is refused permission to sit a public exam, e.g. Standard Grade or Higher, his or her parents may appeal to the school against this decision.

Anyone caught cheating in a public exam is likely to be disqualified and the examination board may decide not to mark any of the candidate's papers. Candidates disqualified for cheating have a right of appeal to the exam board. It is an offence to impersonate someone in an exam. Both the impersonator and the person being impersonated can be charged.

If a candidate does not do as well as expected in an exam, the school may ask for their paper to be checked at the appeal stage to make sure that the marks have been correctly assessed. Certain costs may be involved in this which parents might have to fund.

There is very little that can be done for a candidate who does badly in an exam because of poor teaching or a failure by a teacher to follow the correct procedure – or even the right syllabus. The examining board gives grades based on the candidate's actual performance. If an education authority has been negligent in its education of a pupil, compensation may be available. However, action through the courts for compensation can be costly and has no guarantee of success.

bullying

Schools are under a legal duty to take steps to prevent bullying in school and to publish their policy on dealing with it. It's important that parents and the school are told of any bullying as soon as possible. Schools have a duty to care for their pupils and must act on any evidence of bullying. In serious cases, schools can involve the police. It is possible for a pupil to take legal action against another pupil to put a stop to bullying.

The Scottish Executive has produced two booklets on this subject, *Let's Stop Bullying: Advice for Young People* and *Let's Stop Bullying: Advice for Parents and Families.*

Safety

The education authority has a duty to take reasonable care of pupils while they are under its charge. On a school trip, for example, this can apply for 24 hours a day. The standard of supervision required depends on the nature of the activity and the age or capability of the pupils. Where the action of teachers is called into question, the test the courts apply is whether they were negligent, i.e. have they acted in a way in which no reasonable teacher would have acted?

Schools also have responsibilities for their pupils under health and safety legislation. This is part of the criminal law and is enforced by the Health & Safety Executive.

▮ BRIEF CASE: Bullying

In June 1997, a Sheriff Court sentenced two pupils from a Scottish school to three months youth detention for assault on a fellow pupil who had earlier committed suicide as a result of the assault and other incidents of bullying, including threats issued to her on the day she took her own life.

work

and training

34 part-time work
35 training
39 applying for work
40 contracts
43 health & safety
44 equal rights
47 maternity &
   family rights
48 trade unions
49 losing your job

young citizen's **passport**

INDIVIDUALS
ENGAGING IN
SOCIETY

Citizenship Foundation

part-time work

The law controlling the work of young people below school leaving age varies from one local authority to another.

Under the *Children and Young Persons (Scotland) Act 1937*, each local authority creates its own by-laws giving the terms and conditions for the employment of young people in that area.

These state the kind of work that a young person may, or may not, do and require employers to obtain a permit from the council before employing a child. Although ignored in many areas, the rules also state that, generally speaking, anyone below school leaving age who has a part-time job must have a medical certificate of fitness for work.

Generally, it is only children aged 13 or over who are permitted to work. The only kind of employment children aged 13 or over can be given is light work, such as work in a hairdresser, office, shop (ie shelf stacking), or delivering newspapers. The categories will vary between local authorities.

Restrictions are also imposed on the hours a young person can work on a school day, the hours that can be worked before the start of school and the maximum number of hours that can be worked per week during term-time. These may vary between local authorities.

There are few restrictions on the employment of 16 or 17 year olds. However, people under 18 cannot normally work in a bar, unless they work in a restaurant where drinks are served with meals, or are being trained for the licensing trade under a Modern Apprenticeship scheme. Copies of the by-laws controlling the employment of young people in your area can be obtained from the local library, or the council or education office.

■ BRIEF CASE

A boy of 14, working in a factory making beds, suffered severe injuries when his arm was trapped in an unguarded machine. A court fined his employer £1,000 for failing to fit a guard to the machine and £200 for employing a child. The employer also paid £438 towards the costs of the case.

Employment rights

In 1994, senior judges decided that UK laws unfairly discriminated against part-time workers. As a result, many of the rights of those in part-time jobs (even if it's for only a couple of hours per week) are now the same as those of people in full-time employment.

If you are in part-time work you:

- **are protected by the anti-discrimination laws, regardless of how many hours you work or how long you have worked for your employer;**
- **have the right, if you have worked for your employer for one month, to be given notice if asked to leave and, after two months to receive the terms and conditions of your job, in writing;**
- **are entitled to redundancy pay if you are made redundant and have worked for your employer for at least two years; and**
- **are entitled to claim for unfair dismissal if you have worked for your employer for at least a year, and feel you have been unfairly sacked.**

The *Part-time Workers (Prevention of Less Favourable Treatment) Regulations 2000* state that part-timers must receive the same treatment as full-time workers in relation to their hourly rates of pay, training, holiday, and maternity rights, etc.

training

Youth training

Skillseekers offer work-based training to young people leaving full-time education. The programme is targeted particularly at 16–18 year old school leavers but is open to some young people who have left full-time education who would be able to complete training by the age of 25. All Skillseekers work towards a nationally recognised Scottish Vocational Qualification (SVQ).

Training can last up to three years, but this is flexible and dependent on individual ability, the type of qualification aimed for and the type of training you do.

Alternatively, Modern Apprenticeships offer those aged over 16 paid employment combined with the opportunity to train for jobs at craft, technician and management level. As a Modern Apprentice you will be employed from the very start of your training and receive a wage from your employer. You will receive on-the-job training and assessment and may also be required to attend a college or training centre to study the theory relating to your chosen occupation.

Completion of the Modern Apprenticeship will result in you getting an SVQ at level three or above.

For more information on working and studying in Europe, see European Youth Portal in **contacts**.

training

Pay

You may be taken on as an employee or a work-based Skillseekers trainee, undertaking the programme because you are unemployed and looking for work. As an employee, you will receive at least the minimum wage (see page 41). Apprentices do not qualify for the minimum wage until they are 19 or have completed a year of their apprenticeship, whichever comes later. If you are a trainee, you will receive a training allowance. You can also get payments towards the cost of travel and accommodation, if training away from your home.

Terms and conditions

Whether you are an employee or a work-based trainee, you are entitled to receive written details of the terms and conditions of your training. If you are employed you are covered by all the other rights and benefits mentioned in this chapter.

If you are a work-based trainee you will also be given an individual training plan that will explain:

- **how your training will be organised;**
- **the date when your programme begins and ends;**
- **what time will be spent in the workplace and college or training centre;**
- **details of the SVQ for which you are training.**

If you are not happy with your training, you may be able to transfer to a different programme with the same trainer or with another one. If your trainer cannot finish your training, you should be given the opportunity to transfer to another trainer with a similar training programme.

If you are absent for more than the period specified in your terms and conditions, without permission from your trainer, your training programme will end.

Careers Scotland or your Local Enterprise Company should be able to give you details of apprenticeships in your area.

BRIEF CASE: Karen

Karen applied for an apprenticeship at a garage. She was the best qualified applicant and had already worked in a garage as part of her work experience. At her interview she was asked whether she minded spending all day in a pair of dirty overalls, covered in oil and grease. Karen said she wasn't bothered, but didn't get the job. Karen believed she had been unfairly discriminated against and took her case to an employment tribunal. The tribunal agreed and awarded just over £24,000 for loss of earnings and injury to her feelings.

Equal opportunities

Trainees have the same protection as other workers against unfair discrimination. Help is available at your careers office and the local Citizens' Advice Bureau. For more information, see **equal rights**, page 44.

Health & safety

Your trainer or employer must make sure that the place where you work is safe, and you have a legal responsibility to follow all safety procedures and use equipment in the way instructed.

If you have an accident, or are worried about safety, speak to your supervisor immediately. If you are injured or become ill while training, you should also contact your local Jobcentre Plus office.

Anyone injured while training may be able to claim Industrial Injuries Disablement Benefit. Contact your local Jobcentre Plus office for details.

Problems

When you start training you should be told what to do if you have any problems while on the programme. If you are unhappy with the training you can discuss it with your supervisor or see the careers officer, who may be able to help solve the problem or find you more suitable training.

Non-employed trainees are not entitled to any notice if they are dismissed, nor can they take their case to an employment tribunal if they feel they have been sacked unfairly. But if they are offered another job, they don't need to work out their notice before leaving. Employed trainees or apprentices receive the same legal protection as other employees and should give whatever period of notice is stated in their contract of employment.

This programme is designed to help young people into work, with advice, support, training and work experience. It falls into two categories. The first is for people aged 18–24 who have been claiming Jobseeker's Allowance for six months or more. (Some people, such as lone parents, ex-offenders, those who have just left the armed services and those with a health condition or disability need not wait for the six month qualification period.) The second category is for long-term unemployed people, aged 25 and over.

New Deal for 18-24 year olds is compulsory in the sense that someone who doesn't take up the programme without good reason, stands to lose their right to benefits.

If you are eligible, you will have an appointment with a personal adviser who will explain the programme, give you advice on finding work and monitor progress, based on an action plan that you will be required to draw up. If, at the end of this initial period of up to months, you are not yet in work, your personal adviser will arrange a package of help that might include training, work experience and help with applying for and obtaining work. During this time, you will receive a training allowance equivalent to your Jobseekers' Allowance plus a possible top-up payment of £15.38 per week. If you are on a training or work placement, you have the same legal rights as other employees – but no right to stay in the post after six months.

If you do not find work at the end of this period, you will continue to receive Jobseeker's Allowance and your personal adviser will carry on helping you to find a job.

The New Deal Information Line is on 0845 606 2626, open 7 days a week, from 7am – 11pm.

use the law with care try talking first

Applications

Read through the application form before starting to fill it in. Draft your longer answers in rough, until you are happy with what you have written.

All the information you give should be correct. An employer is usually entitled to dismiss someone who is deliberately misleading on their application form or at interview.

Your CV

Some adverts for jobs tell you to send for an application form, others will ask for a letter with your curriculum vitae, usually known as a C.V. This is something that you write or type, giving personal details, qualifications, experience, and interests. Make several copies and don't forget to keep one yourself.

Referees

You will need the names of two people who are prepared to act as your referees, to write a short report or reference about you for an employer. One referee is usually your last employer, or the head teacher or year tutor in your school.

Interviews

If you've not been to the office or building before, leave yourself extra time to find it; or go round and find out where it is beforehand. If you can't make the appointment, phone or write to explain and ask for a more convenient time.

Have a few questions ready to ask – about what the course or job involves. If they offer you a place or job, before you accept try to think if there's anything else you need to know. If there is, ask.

contracts

Everyone at work has a contract – whether full or part-time, permanent or fixed term.

A contract is another word for the agreement between you and your employer, spelling out the arrangements that will affect your work – such as pay, hours, the sort of job you will do, holidays and the notice you have to give, or you can expect to receive, when your employment comes to an end.

Terms and conditions in writing

If you are to be employed for more than one month, your employer must give you a written statement within two months of starting work, setting out the terms and conditions of your job.

Some of the things this statement should contain are:

- your job title and place of work;
- your starting date;
- your rate of pay, and details of how and when you will be paid;
- your hours of work;
- your holidays and holiday pay;
- arrangements for sick pay and pension;
- details of the firm's disciplinary procedures, and how complaints at work are dealt with; and
- the amount of notice that you or your employer must give if your contract is to be ended.

People often think that contracts have to be written down – they don't. They can be agreed verbally – but it's a good idea to have things in writing, in case there's disagreement about what you're expected to do.

Check your contract carefully. Make sure you agree with what it says and that it covers everything you are being asked to do. If it is different from the agreement made at your interview, point this out. Keep safe all pay slips, letters and papers you are given by your employer.

Take care

If you agree to do something on a regular basis that is not written into your contract – like working on a Saturday – you may be, in law, agreeing to a new term or condition of work. If you decide later that working every Saturday is not a good idea, your boss may be entitled to insist that you continue. By turning up for work six days a week, you may have actually changed your contract by your conduct.

use the law with care try talking first

Pay

Your wages will either be agreed between you and your boss or else based on rates agreed between employers and the trade union. Either way, your employer must give you a detailed written pay statement each time you are paid, showing exactly what you are being paid and how much is being taken off in tax, national insurance etc. It is up to your employer to choose how you are paid. This can be by cash, cheque, or straight into your bank account.

Your rate of sick pay must be explained in your contract. It will probably say either that you will be paid at your standard rate for a certain length of time, or that you will be given statutory sick pay. This is set each year by the Department for Work and Pensions and is usually lower than your normal pay. If you are off sick for four or more days in a row (including Sundays and bank holidays) you will receive statutory sick pay from your employer for up to 28 weeks. You don't have to claim statutory sick pay, just follow your employer's rules for notifying sickness.

You can check what you should receive in leaflets available from Department for Work and Pension offices and libraries.

MINIMUM PAY

Under the *National Minimum Wage Act 1998*, the minimum rate payable to 16 and 17 year olds, who are above compulsory school age is currently £3.30 per hour. Those aged 18–21 are entitled to receive £4.45 per hour and for people aged 22 and over, the rate is £5.35 per hour, unless they are in the first six months of a new job or on an accredited training course. These rates are revised in October each year and will next change in October 2007.

If you are being paid less than the national minimum wage, you have a legal right to raise it directly with your manager and, if you are a member of a trade union, should get in touch with them.

An employer can be fined for paying below the minimum wage and must not treat an employee unfairly for raising the matter.

If your employer fails to grant your legal rights, you may take your case to an employment tribunal. Further help is available from the National Minimum Wage Helpline, see contacts for details.

Hours

Your hours of work will normally be agreed between you and your employer, although these are limited by law in certain ways for reasons of health and safety.

The Working Time Regulations set maximum limits of eight hours a day or 40 hours a week for young workers ie those over minimum school leaving age but under 18. These hours cannot be averaged and you can only work longer

contracts

than this in certain circumstances where there is no adult available to work instead and it will not adversely affect your training needs. For workers 18 and over, the maximum working week of 48 hours, including overtime, can be averaged over 17 weeks. You can agree to do more than this, but your employer cannot pressurise you to do so. You are also entitled to:

- **a rest break of 20 minutes when you work for more than six hours at a time (or 30 minutes every four hours if you are under 18); and**
- **at least eleven consecutive hours off in any 24 hour period (twelve hours off, if you are under 18).**

Workers who are under 18 may not ordinarily work between 10pm and 6am. Some night work is allowed in certain jobs, such as farm work, catering, working in a pub, restaurant or hotel, working in a bakery, newspaper delivery and retail trading. However, an adult must supervise the work and rest periods must be given. Workers who believe that the hours they are expected to work do not follow the regulations, can take their case to an employment tribunal.

HOLIDAYS

The *Working Time Regulations* give most people over 16 the right to at least four weeks' paid holiday a year. During the first year of employment, you have the right to take one twelfth of your annual holiday entitlement for each month worked. Some jobs are not fully covered by the Regulations, for example those in the police and armed forces.

rules and regulations

Computer use

A variety of legislation entitles employers to set reasonable rules for their workers who use e-mail and the Internet at work.

They can forbid employees from using work systems for personal e-mail and Internet use, either at all, or during work time. However, employees should be informed that checks of this kind might be made. An employer who opens an employee's emails without a good business reason could well be infringing that person's right to privacy (see Human Rights, page 124).

E-mail files may however be opened without an employee's consent in extreme circumstances, to check, for example, whether the law has been broken.

use the law with care try talking first

Safety

Employers have a legal duty to take care of the safety of their staff. If they don't, they are breaking the *Health and Safety at Work Act 1974*.

This means that the equipment that you use must not be dangerous or defective, and that the people you work with must work safely and responsibly.

Your duty is to follow safety regulations and to take care of your own and other people's safety.

If you work for a firm where there are five or more employees, your boss must give you details of the health and safety arrangements in writing.

If you are worried about health and safety, raise the matter with your supervisor. Your employer may not dismiss you or treat you unfairly for raising genuine concerns, as long as you follow the right procedures. If you remain concerned, contact the local offices of the Health and Safety Executive. Your local Citizens' Advice Bureau will be able to tell you how to do this.

■ BRIEF CASE: Irene

Irene worked as an education welfare officer. One day she was viciously attacked and robbed while doing her job. One of the things stolen was her identity card which was then used to gain entry to the homes of pupils she worked with. This led to her being transferred. However, in her new school she was provided with a dark and isolated classroom. She felt the room was an unsafe working environment and she ultimately resigned when nothing was done to move her to a different area of the building. She decided to take her case to an employment tribunal to claim constructive dismissal. The tribunal agreed that her dismissal was unfair – an employer has a duty to provide a working environment that is suitable for employees to work in.

brief case

health & safety

Accidents

If you are injured at work, report the matter to your supervisor straightaway and, unless the injury is very small, see a doctor. Make a note of what happened, get the names of any witnesses, check to see whether you are entitled to any welfare benefits and get legal advice from either your trade union or a solicitor. You may be entitled to compensation for your injuries.

Using a computer screen

If you have a problem with your eyes that you think might be due to using display screen equipment at work, your employer has a duty to arrange for you to have an eyesight test if you ask for one, and to do whatever they reasonably can at work to reduce further problems. This is all part of a general requirement for employers to check on the health and safety risks to people using computer screens at work, contained in the *Health and Safety (Display Screen Equipment) Regulations 1992*.

■ **BRIEF CASE: Gary**

Gary, 18, worked in a butcher's and was cutting meat when his hand slipped and he cut off the top of two fingers. His boss had often told him to use a special guard – but most people at work ignored this, so Gary didn't bother either. Gary was awarded damages in court because his employer did not make sure that he was working in the right way, but they were reduced by a third because he hadn't followed the safety instructions.

FINGER LICKING SAUSAGES

Only the best will do

equal rights

Discrimination

Over the last 40 years, the law has gradually provided more and more protection against discrimination at work. Discrimination law applies to all aspects of work including applications, pensions, and references that might be given when you have left.

Sex

Under the *Sex Discrimination Act 1975*, it is against the law to treat a person less favourably because of their sex. In narrow circumstances an employer can have a defence, for example, when a female is a genuine requirement for the job. This includes certain acting and modelling roles, and those that may involve close physical contact with an individual. The *Equal Pay Act 1970* gives women and men rights to equal pay for the same or similar work.

use the law with care **try talking first**

Race It is against the law to discriminate against someone because of their colour, race, nationality, or ethnic origin. This is covered by the *Race Relations Act 1976*, and applies equally to all racial groups.

There are certain circumstances when race discrimination is not against the law, for example, when a person's race or ethnic group is seen as a 'genuine occupational qualification', such as in a restaurant serving food from a particular country or region.

Disability It is against the law, under the *Disability Discrimination Act 1995*, for any employer to treat a person with a disability less favourably than someone without, unless it can be justified for a sound business reason. Employers are required to make reasonable adjustments to the working environment in order to enable a person with disabilities to be employed.

Religion Under the *Employment Equality (Religion or Belief) Regulations 2003*, employers should not treat an employee less favourably than others because of their religion or beliefs. Nor should employers have rules and practices that put someone at a disadvantage because of their religion. For example, employers generally do not have the right to compel a person to dress in a particular way that is against their religion or system of beliefs, unless there is a very strong business reason to do so.

Sexuality Since 2003, it has been against the law to discriminate against someone at work because of their sexuality. Under the *Employment Equality (Sexual Orientation) Regulations 2003*, employers may not treat gay, lesbian, or bisexual employees less favourably than others. The law applies to all organisations and business, whatever their size.

Age Under the Employment Equality (Age) Regulations 2006, it is now against the law to discriminate against someone at work because of their age. Generally speaking a person should not be turned down for a job because they are too old or too young, and employers should not advertise jobs for particular age groups.

■ BRIEF CASE: Eugene

Eugene suffered constant racist taunts from other workers on the building site where he worked, and the management did little to stop it. They said that "black bastard" and "nigger" were words often used on sites. The tribunal decided that Eugene had been directly discriminated against. He was awarded £2,000 damages.

equal rights

BRIEF CASE: Susan

Help and advice

If you feel you have been a victim of unfair discrimination at work, you can get help from your local Citizens' Advice Bureau, Law Centre or trade union. Advice and information on racial matters is available from the Commission for Racial Equality, on sex discrimination from the Equal Opportunities Commission and on disability matters from the Disability Rights Commission, see **contacts**.

If you can't sort out things informally, you may be advised to take your complaint to an employment tribunal. This must be done within three months (or six months, if it is a claim under the Equal Pay Act). If you win, the tribunal can award damages to compensate you for the losses you have suffered. You may be able to settle your case without the need to go to court but, if not, be prepared for a long and difficult battle, and remember to take legal advice.

Harrassment at work

The law also allows employees to make a claim against their employer if they face harassment at work. Like discrimination, this can be because of their sex, race, disability, religion, sexual orientation or age.

Harassment refers to behaviour that the person on the receiving end finds intimidating, offensive or demeaning. Examples might include:

- **unwanted advances or physical contact;**
- **insulting remarks;**
- **comments on a person's looks.**

It is an employer's duty to take steps to prevent these kinds of things from happening. If you face difficulties of this kind it's usually better, if you can, to try

> Susan, a train driver on the London Underground, was forced to hand in her notice when new shift rosters meant that it was impossible for her to work and look after her three year old child. She took her case to an employment tribunal, complaining of sex discrimination. The tribunal decided that the new working arrangements indirectly discriminated against women because more women were single parents.

to sort things out personally. But if the harassment continues, don't be afraid to complain using your employer's grievance procedure. It's not always easy to prove in court, but judges are now prepared to award damages when the victim can show that they have suffered some disadvantage or injury to their feelings from the harassment.

maternity & family rights

Maternity rights

All women at work who are expecting a baby or adopting a child have certain minimum legal rights. Some employers provide more than these. You can check your position from your contract.

Time off with pay for antenatal care

This applies to full and part-time workers, and it makes no difference how long you have worked for your employer. Your employer cannot insist that you make up the time, or that you take the appointment in your free time.

Maternity leave

From 1st October 2006 pregnant women whose baby is due on or after 1st April 2007 are entitled to 52 weeks of maternity leave no matter how long they have worked for their employer, and whether they are full or part-time. All benefits, except pay, listed in your contract, continue throughout your maternity leave – including medical insurance, pension, and even a company car, if you have one. You can agree to work on up to 10 days during your maternity leave to keep in touch with your workplace.

Correct procedures

If you don't follow the correct procedures in applying for maternity leave, you risk losing the right to return to your job after your baby is born. For example, you must give notice to your employer by the end of the 15th week before the baby is due and you must give 8 weeks' notice of your intention to return to work. The personnel department at work, your trade union, or local Citizens' Advice Bureau can explain what you need to do.

You are entitled, from April 2007, to maternity pay for the first nine months of your maternity leave including the time you take off before your baby is born. This will probably be lower than your usual rate, unless it says otherwise in your contract. If you are on a low income or have not worked for long enough to qualify for maternity pay, you may still be entitled to a maternity allowance from the Benefits Agency.

A guide to maternity rights is available free from the Department of Trade and Industry, see **contacts**.

The standard rate of maternity pay and the maternity allowance is £112.75 per week, or ninety per cent of your average weekly earnings, if less.

maternity & family rights

Paternity leave

If you have become a dad and have worked for your employer for 26 weeks by the 15th week before your baby is due, you may have the right to two weeks' paid paternity leave. The standard rate of paternity pay is the same as for maternity pay. In the future, the amount of paternity leave available to new dads will increase to 26 weeks and a date for this is to be announced.

Parental leave

Both parents can take up to 13 weeks' unpaid parental leave over the first five years of their child's life provided they have worked for their employer for at least a year.

Parents of disabled children are entitled to 18 weeks' unpaid leave over the first 18 years of the child's life.

Time off

Regardless of how long you have worked for your employer, you have the right to take unpaid time off for urgent family problems, such as an accident or the sudden illness of someone who depends on you for their care, but you must give your employer the reasons for your absence as soon as possible.

You may only take a reasonable amount of time. If your employer refuses, you can complain to an employment tribunal.

Right to request flexible working

If you have 26 weeks' service and are a parent, stepparent, adopter, foster carer or guardian of a child who is under six years old or a disabled child who is under 18 years old, you have the right to request flexible working hours for the purpose of looking after your child. From April 2007 adults caring for other adults – including their spouses, parents or partners – can also request flexible working hours.

trade unions

Membership

It is up to you whether you join a trade union. Trade unions don't only negotiate wages for their members. They also give advice, inform members of their rights and act on their behalf over difficulties with their employer. An employer must not sack someone for either belonging or not belonging to a trade union.

Not all employers want to work with unions. But, if there are 21 or more people working for an employer, a trade union may be able to force the employer to recognise the union and to negotiate with them.

Industrial action

If you take industrial action – for example, by stopping work – you may be breaking your contract.

However, if the strike has been lawfully organised and correctly balloted, your employer is not entitled to dismiss you for taking part. This is automatically unfair and you may have a case for compensation. But you cannot claim unfair dismissal if you are sacked for taking part in an unofficial strike.

use the law with care try talking first

If you're sacked or made redundant, your legal rights mainly depend on how long you have been working for the firm.

Notice Unless you have done something very serious and committed what's known in law as gross misconduct – such as theft or fighting – your boss should not sack you on the spot. Your contract should state the notice to which you are entitled, and this usually depends on how long you have been working for your employer.

After one month's employment, either side should give one week's notice. After two years' employment, your employer should give you two weeks' notice, three weeks' after three years, and so on, up to twelve weeks' notice for employment which has lasted twelve years or more.

However, your notice period might be longer if this is stated in your contract, and your employer may decide to pay you instead of letting you work out your notice. Before dismissing you, your employer must follow certain procedures designed to promote discussion.

Reasons in writing If you are fired by your employer, for whom you have worked for more than one year, you can ask for a written statement of the reasons for your dismissal. Your employer must provide this within 14 days. If you are dismissed during pregnancy or maternity leave, you should automatically receive a written statement.

Redundancy This happens when an employer no longer needs the job done for which you were employed. Your rights mainly depend on your age and how long you have worked for the firm.

If you are made redundant, you have a right to redundancy pay, if you:

- **have worked for your employer for a continuous period of at least two years; and**
- **have not unreasonably turned down an offer of another job from your employer.**

If your employer has gone bust, you may be able to get a redundancy payment from the Redundancy Payments Service.

If you are made redundant, get advice from your trade union, Citizens' Advice Bureau or a solicitor as soon as possible. If you feel that the way you were chosen for redundancy was unfair or unreasonable, or that your employer has failed to consult adequately with you, you may also be able to claim unfair dismissal.

Information Your rights to a redundancy payment are explained on the Department of Trade and Industry's website, see **contacts**.

losing your job

UNFAIR DISMISSAL

If you feel that you have been unfairly dismissed, and have worked for your employer continuously for a year or more, you can make a complaint to an employment tribunal.

Even if you've not been sacked, but leave your job because of the behaviour of your employer, you may have a claim for unfair dismissal. This is known in law as constructive dismissal, but will only be successful if you can show that your employer has broken your employment contract. If you are thinking of resigning because of this, keep a record of what is happening and, before you hand in your notice, write to your employer explaining your reasons for leaving.

Take legal advice before you make a claim for unfair dismissal. Your trade union, local Citizens' Advice Bureau or a solicitor can help. If you are unhappy about your dismissal, don't delay in seeking assistance. As a basic rule you only have three months in which to make a complaint.

If the tribunal agrees that your dismissal was unfair, your employer will probably be ordered to pay you a sum in compensation. This is based on the amount of redundancy you would be entitled to, plus a figure for compensation. The maximum basic redundancy award is £9,300 and the maximum figure for compensation is £60,600.

There are no limits to the damages you can receive if you lose your job because of discrimination or if you are dismissed unfairly or selected for redundancy for reasons connected with health and safety matters.

■ BRIEF CASE: Sacked!

Jeannette's son was ill in the night and Jeannette overslept the next morning. When she arrived late at the video rental company where she worked, she was sacked. She explained what had happened, but her boss took no notice. Jeannette took her case to an employment tribunal, who decided that she had been unfairly dismissed, as she had not been given a warning or a second chance.

■ BRIEF CASE: Redundant!

Business was bad and Dean was made redundant from his job at a petrol station. He was given £520 redundancy pay, but soon realised that his job was now being done by the boss's son. Dean hadn't been redundant at all, and so won his claim for unfair dismissal.

money

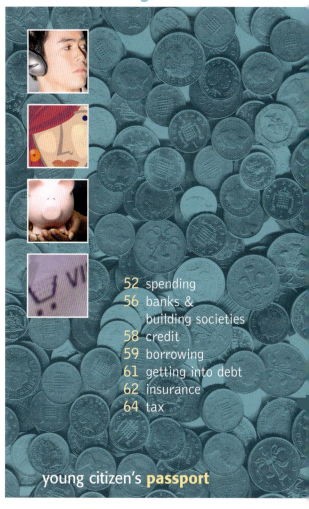

52 spending
56 banks &
   building societies
58 credit
59 borrowing
61 getting into debt
62 insurance
64 tax

young citizen's **passport**

INDIVIDUALS
ENGAGING IN
SOCIETY

Citizenship Foundation

spending

When you buy something from a shop or pay for a service (like a train fare or haircut) you are making an agreement, known in law as a *contract*.

The contract means that, in return for the money that you pay, the goods you buy should do everything you can reasonably expect and, in particular, all that the seller and manufacturer claim.

Once a contract has been agreed, neither side can change it on their own. Some shops allow customers to opt out of their contract by agreeing to exchange unwanted items or by providing a refund, as long as goods are returned in mint condition with the receipt. Shops don't have to do this by law, unless it was promised as part of the contract.

But what about your rights if the goods you have bought are faulty?

The Sale of Goods Act

The law applying to most everyday purchases is the *Sale of Goods Act 1979*. This was updated in 2003 to provide new protection for consumers. It says that when you buy goods from a shop or trader, they must …

…be of satisfactory quality

This means that they must be free from faults and not scratched or damaged, and equally applies to goods bought in a sale. However, this rule does not apply if the fault was pointed out by the sales assistant or if you inspected the item and had a good opportunity to discover the fault.

Second-hand goods bought from a shop or trader must also be of satisfactory quality. This protection does not apply if you bought the goods privately (e.g. through a 'small ad') – when the buyer is responsible for deciding the quality of what she or he wants to buy.

…match the description

The goods must be the same as the description on the packaging or advertisement, or given by the assistant at the time of sale. A bracelet marked solid silver, must be just that.

This rule also applies to second-hand goods, including those sold privately.

…be fit for all their intended purposes

This means that they must do what the seller, packaging or advertisements claim. A watch sold as waterproof should not stop if you forget to take it off in the shower.

use the law with care try talking first

GETTING IT RIGHT

If you're buying something expensive, and want to do some research beforehand, Which? magazine, available in most libraries, gives a guide to the price and performance of many products. You can also go to a shop and ask just to see an item, without buying it. If you decide to make a purchase, keep the receipt in case you have a complaint.

Services too

Dry cleaners, shoe repairers, hairdressers, travel agents and many others provide a service – and you are protected by law if that service is inadequate.

Under the *Supply of Goods and Services Act 1982*, a service must be provided:

- **with reasonable care and skill;**
- **within a reasonable time; and**
- **for a reasonable charge.**

Problems?

Problems are less likely to occur if certain things are agreed before the work is started. How much will it cost? How long will it take? What happens if the work can't be finished? Try to sort these out first.

Handle your complaint just as you would were it for faulty goods. Don't be afraid to seek advice. Help is available from your local Citizens' Advice Bureau or consumer advice centre.

Some trades, such as travel agents, garages, dry cleaners, shoe sellers etc. have their own associations laying down a code of practice or standards. These have no legal standing, but the associations can put pressure on their members to treat customers' complaints in a reasonable way. It may be worth a try, and your local library can give you the address to contact. In some situations, an Ombudsman may be able to help, see **contacts** for details.

spending

PUT DOWNS

Some businesses will do as much as they can to help you with a problem over something you have bought; others may claim that there is nothing they can do. Don't give up if the shop tries to get out of its legal obligations...

...we'll send it back to the workshop

Only if you want them to. If you act reasonably quickly you can choose whether to ask for a full or partial refund, compensation or to have the goods repaired or replaced (if that is a practical option). If the goods have developed a fault in the first six months it is assumed they were faulty when you bought them (unless the shop can prove otherwise).

... you'll have to take it up with the manufacturer

Wrong. You bought the goods from the shop and your contract was with them, not with a manufacturer on the other side of the world. If the goods genuinely don't work, the shop has not kept its side of the contract and you have a right to your money back. Shops normally have to accept responsibility to you for the manufacturer's claims.

...we'll give you a credit note

No. If the goods are faulty, you're entitled to your money back. You don't have to accept a credit note if you don't want to. If you do accept a credit note, check where and when you can use it – some credit notes must be used within a fixed time and only in exchange for certain goods or services.

...sorry, it's out of guarantee

This can be tricky. A major problem with an expensive computer three months after the guarantee has run out means a large repair bill. Raise it with the dealer and ask to talk to the manager. Produce the documentation and use the manufacturer's literature (which probably stresses reliability and quality) to point out that it is not reasonable to expect a failure after such a short period. There's no hard and fast law about what is reasonable in terms of a product failure. It depends on the circumstances.

...we don't give refunds on sale goods

Wrong. Unless the fault was pointed out to you or was something you should have seen when you bought them, goods bought in sales carry all the protection of the *Sale of Goods Act 1979*.

...we'll give you a replacement

Only if that's what you want. However, if by now the fault has led you to decide that you don't really want the product after all, you are entitled to your money back – not a replacement. It's up to you to choose what to do.

The small claims court

If you cannot get any satisfaction over a problem with faulty goods or poor service, you can write to the person concerned warning them that you will try to recover the money they owe you by taking your case to the small claims court (strictly known as the small claims procedure in the sheriff court). You need to be 16 years old or more. Younger people need to ask their parent or guardian to bring the case on their behalf. This is a less formal way of settling disputes where the value is less than £750 (or up to £1,500 in what is known as a "summary cause"), at a fraction of the normal cost, in which a judge hears your case without the expense of having to instruct your own lawyer. You can get more details from your local sheriff court (under Courts in the phone book or at www.scotcourts.gov.uk), the Citizens' Advice Bureau or a consumer advice centre.

Finding it's wrong

If you are not satisfied with something that you have bought...

> Stop using it straightaway and take it back, with the receipt and guarantee (if you have one), to the shop where you bought it. It strengthens your case if you can do this as soon as possible. Your contract was with the shop, not the manufacturer, so it is the shop's responsibility to deal with your complaint. Even if you have lost the receipt, the contract still exists.

> Before you take the goods back, decide what you are going to say and what you would like the shop to do. Do you want your money back, or will you accept a repair or a replacement item?

> Think about your legal position. A faulty stop button on a personal stereo means that it is not of satisfactory quality. Don't be afraid to use the law when making your case.

> If the shop assistant doesn't help, ask for someone more senior.

> If you bought the goods by mail order or from a shop some distance away, it's easier to telephone or write. Keep a copy of all letters, send a photocopy of your receipt (keep the original), and if you talk on the phone get the name of the person you spoke to. Make a brief note of the conversation.

Buying over the phone or on the Internet

The same rules apply here as when you buy from a shop, but the trader must give you some basic information like the name and address of the person you are dealing with and, in most cases, you should be given the chance to cancel your order within seven days.

You can get more details from the Office of Fair Trading or a Citizens' Advice Bureau; see **contacts**.

banks and building societies

Although there is no minimum legal age for someone to have a bank account, most banks offer accounts to young people aged eleven and over. These tend to be fairly basic, and a regular account is normally only available if you are 18 or over (or 16 or 17 with a steady income or an adult who will act as guarantor).

WHY HAVE AN ACCOUNT?

- many employers will only pay wages into an account;
- an account is needed for a student loan;
- the money can earn interest;
- regular accounts come with a cheque book and card to pay for things;
- you can pay cheques other people give you into an account.

CHOOSING A BANK OR BUILDING SOCIETY

You will probably want to know:
- whether it has a branch near you and offers on-line banking;
- whether there are convenient cash points;
- about services offered and charges;
- what interest is paid on the money in your account. There will be leaflets on this, or you can ask a member of staff; and
- about special offers for young people.

Don't be persuaded by offers or gifts if the services and charges are not as good as other banks or building societies.

The two main types are current accounts and savings accounts.

Current accounts

A current account is the normal account for day-to-day transactions. You pay in money, such as your wages or student loan, which you can draw out as you please. If you are 18 or over, you usually get a chequebook and a cheque guarantee card, which allows you to pay for and take away things, with a signed cheque.

You'll receive a regular bank statement – usually every month – showing the amounts that have been paid in and withdrawn from your account and your overall balance.

Cheque books and guarantee cards

A chequebook contains a number of cheques with your name on. The person you give a cheque to pays it into their bank account, and after a few days the money is taken (debited) from your account and added (or credited) to theirs.

If you haven't enough money in your current account to cover the value of the cheque you have written, the bank may refuse to honour your cheque and it will bounce.

You may also be given a cheque guarantee card. This guarantees that the bank will honour your cheque up to the amount stated on the card – usually £50 or £100. If there isn't enough money in your account to

cover the value of the cheques you have written with your cheque guarantee card, you'll go overdrawn and may have to pay bank charges and interest. Strictly speaking it is an offence to write a cheque when you know there is not enough money in your account to cover it, unless you have the permission of your bank to do so. Don't keep your chequebook and guarantee card together.

Cashcards These allow you to take money out of your current account from a cash machine, using a confidential personal identification number (PIN). Never keep a record of this number with your card.

Debit cards Your debit card allows you to buy things without writing a cheque or using cash. You can also use it to pay for goods over the telephone or on the internet. Your account is automatically debited with the amount you have spent. However, it can take a while (sometimes a few days) for payments to show on your balance. You can only go overdrawn with a debit card if you have the bank's agreement, otherwise you will be charged a fee. Many debit cards double as a cheque guarantee and cash card.

What do I do if someone gives me a cheque? Look to see that it is correctly written – that it is for the right amount, that it has been signed, and is not 'post-dated' (has a future date on).

Pay the cheque into your account as soon as possible, using a paying-in slip. Banks do not usually accept cheques more than six months old.

banks and building societies

Savings accounts A savings account provides a higher rate of interest. Most do not come with a chequebook or plastic card, and some have restrictions on when you can withdraw your money. However, you will still be able to take out your money if your really have to, but will probably lose some of the extra interest.

If you keep money in your savings account while you are overdrawn on your current account or have a loan, you may find the interest you are paying is higher than the interest that you earn on your savings account.

What about tax on the interest I earn? Interest earned on bank and building society accounts is usually paid after tax has been deducted from it. Unless you have a high income, that is normally the end of the matter, and there is no more tax to pay; see **tax** page 64. If you are not a taxpayer (because your earnings are not high enough), you can either get the tax back by contacting a tax office or you can choose to have there interest paid to you without tax being deducted. Your bank or building society will have the forms for you to complete that allow them to do this.

credit

Plastic cards These cards can be very useful, but cause difficulties when people are not careful how they are used. Credit and store cards are not usually issued to people below the age of 18.

Credit cards Like debit cards, credit cards allow people to buy goods and services from a huge range of shops and other suppliers, in person, over the phone or on the Internet.

Credit cards enable the shop to be paid straightaway, but the customer is not billed until sometime later. This means that the customer is being lent the money to buy the goods by the firm issuing the credit card.

If you apply for a card, the bank will check out your creditworthiness. A spending limit will be set on the

use the law with care try talking first

account. A fee will be charged if you go over this, and the card may be cancelled.

Each month you will receive a statement, showing how much you have spent, how much is owed, and the minimum payment that must be made. If you do not pay your bill in full, you will be charged interest. If you make no payment at all, you will be charged a further penalty.

You can compare the costs of different cards by looking at the Annual Percentage Rate (APR), which is the rate of interest charged by the firm issuing the credit card. The lower the APR, the lower the cost of borrowing.

Some types of borrowing on a credit card are more expensive than others. Using your credit card to withdraw cash is more expensive than using it to buy goods and there is no interest-free period. This means that interest builds up on the cash from the moment you take it out.

Store cards These are credit cards issued by department stores, clothes and sports shops.

You are sent a regular statement showing how much you have spent, and what you owe. You have to pay off some cards in full at the end of each month. With others, you can pay a fixed minimum amount each time, with the rest being carried forward and appearing on your next statement. Interest is charged on the amount you haven't paid off. These charges are often higher than other types of credit card. You can check the store card's APR and compare it to your credit card.

borrowing

Borrowing from a bank or building society A bank or building society lends money either through allowing an overdraft or by making a loan.

Overdrafts A person becomes overdrawn when they spend more money than they have in their bank account. The most expensive overdraft is an unauthorised one – which is run up without the agreement of the bank. Interest is paid on the amount overdrawn, and charges are added on top.

If you ever find yourself in this situation, it is important to get in touch with the bank as soon as you can.

If you need to go overdrawn, you can usually arrange with your bank an authorised overdraft up to an agreed amount. Interest may be charged. Students may be offered interest free overdrafts.

borrowing and credit

LOANS

A loan is an arrangement with your bank – or other financial institution – under which you are lent a specific amount of money. You enter into a contract for the loan. This will be for a set period, with an agreed rate of interest and time over which you have to repay the full amount. If you are under 16 it is very unlikely that you will be able to get a bank loan, as contracts with people under 16 are not usually binding so the bank will be taking too big a risk.

A loan is usually a better way of borrowing money than running up large debts on a credit card, but it is important to check that the repayment terms are affordable.

Buying goods by instalments – credit or hire purchase

You can often buy more expensive goods (cars, hi-fi systems, TVs) by instalment – that is, by paying only part of the price at the time of purchase, and paying the rest later. This is known as buying on credit or on tick. Sometimes credit is available interest free, but credit is normally an expensive way of paying for things. It is always a good idea to check the charges (the APR) that are being made .

Hire purchase is a special form of buying on credit. Technically the shop sells the goods to a finance company and you pay to "hire" them over an agreed period. When you have paid off what you owe you make a small final payment to purchase the goods (hence "hire purchase"). Only then do you become the owner.

Second thoughts

If you signed a credit deal at home (or away from the shop or business premises) you have a right to cancel if you act quickly. You will be sent a second copy of the agreement that will tell you how to cancel if you want to. If you signed the agreement on business premises then it's much harder to cancel unless the form has to be sent away to the credit company for its signature. Then you can withdraw as long as you tell them before they have signed up.

use the law with care try talking first

People get into debt for all sorts of reasons, often through no fault of their own. They may find they owe money to several different people and are tempted to borrow more to pay off some of these debts. This often becomes even more expensive.

You know it's getting serious when you start getting badgered to make repayments by the people you owe money to – your "creditors" – and you can't meet all the demands.

What to do

• **Don't ignore the problem:** it won't go away and will get worse the longer you leave it. You can get help and, in most cases, you can take control.

• **Draw up a budget:** list all the money you owe and the people to whom it is owed; what your income and reasonable living expenses are; and see how much you can afford to pay back.

• **List your debts in their order of priority:** at the top are those where non payment can have really serious consequences – like losing your flat or home; having the electricity or gas cut off, or where non payment is a criminal offence (like council tax and your TV licence). You should aim to pay these off first and then work out what's left over for the others, treating them equally.

• **Contact all your creditors:** go and see them or write or phone; explain the position and show them your budget. Discuss with them what you can reasonably pay. Usually they will be prepared to negotiate an agreement with you as this improves their chances of getting paid. You may be able to agree to pay by instalments or, for a period of time, just to pay off the interest on your loan.

• **Don't borrow more without getting advice:** there are lots of people prepared to lend you more to pay off earlier debts. They are sometimes called loan-sharks. They will probably charge very high rates of interest making it even more difficult for you to get out of debt. They won't be nearly as easy to deal with if you can't keep up your repayments.

HELP

You can get help and advice from experts. Try the National Debtline, tel 0808 808 4000, www.nationaldebtline.co.uk or a Citizens' Advice Bureau, see contacts.

insurance

Insurance is a way of protecting yourself and your property from an unexpected loss or mishap. You can insure yourself against almost anything – losing your possessions in a fire, having them stolen or damaged, or having to face unexpected medical bills on holiday abroad. If you drive a car or motorcycle, you must be insured by law, see travel and transport, page 101. In return for a premium – an agreed amount of money you pay each month or year – an insurance company will, if the worst does happen, pay you compensation for the losses or damage that you insured against.

Buying insurance

There are two ways of obtaining insurance. You can either deal directly with the company, or go to a broker. Most large insurance companies have offices in the major towns and cities. Their numbers are in the Yellow Pages or local phone book. You can often deal directly with them and arrange your insurance cover by phone or over the Internet.

Insurance brokers are agents who can help you choose an insurer and arrange the policy for you. They don't usually charge you for this, but instead make their money from the insurance company that you have decided to use.

All the information you give should be as accurate as possible. Questions must be answered truthfully, and any other information that could be relevant should also be given. If it's not, the insurance policy will be invalid.

Keep a copy of any form that you complete, and when you renew your insurance (usually done each year) don't forget to tell the insurance company about anything that has changed that might affect your insurance position.

use the law with care try talking first

THE WORDS THEY USE:

Broker

An agent who can help you choose and apply for insurance.

Cover

Insurance against loss or damage.

Cover note

A temporary document showing that you have insurance cover, usually sent out while the official certificate is being prepared.

Excess

The amount you will have to pay towards the cost of your claim.

No claims bonus

The discount you are given on your premium if you haven't made a claim.

Policy

The document setting out the terms and conditions of your insurance.

Premium

The amount you pay for your insurance.

Quotation

A statement of the amount you will have to pay for the insurance you asked for.

tax

Income tax

Money paid in income tax is used to pay for services provided by the state – such as health, education, defence etc. Everyone who earns or receives income over a certain amount in a year pays income tax and, generally speaking, the more you earn, the more you pay. As well as earnings from full and part-time work, tips and bonuses, tax is also paid on interest from savings with banks, building societies and some National Savings accounts, on Income Support and on profits from a business and dividends from shares.

PAYE

Your employer will usually take the tax from your earnings each time you are paid and pass the money on to the tax authorities, called the Inland Revenue. Everyone is entitled to receive a certain amount of money on which they pay no tax at all. This is called a personal allowance, which, for a single person in 2007/2008, is £5,225. Income tax is paid only when your income rises above this. There are other allowances which may be available, e.g. for the cost of tools or special clothing if they are not provided by your employer. If you are on a training programme, your grant in most cases is not taxable.

Part-time workers should not have tax deducted from their pay, unless their income is above £100 a week. If you are a student with a holiday job, ask your employer for a form P38(S) if you think your total taxable income for the year (including earnings and Income Support), will be less than the basic personal allowance, i.e. £5,225. Fill in the form, return it to your employer, and you should then be paid without tax being deducted.

If you have been working and paying tax, but believe your total income for the year will be less than £5,225 ask for form P50 from your local tax office, and return it completed with your P45 from your employer. The Inland Revenue publishes free booklets on tax, obtainable from your library or nearest tax office (under Inland Revenue in the phone book). The Taxpayer's Charter outlines the service you are entitled to expect from staff at the Inland Revenue.

Failure to complete your tax forms correctly can mean extra interest payments and even fines. The Inland Revenue runs a telephone helpline, giving information and advice on tax, see **contacts**.

Tax credits

Working Tax Credits and Child Tax Credits are available to those on low incomes to top up earnings.

NATIONAL INSURANCE

Almost everybody in Britain who is in paid work must pay National Insurance contributions. This money is used to help run the National Health Service and to provide benefits and pensions.

It is generally taken directly from the money that you earn. Everyone has their own NI number, which they receive just before they reach 16. Your NI number is used to record all your NI contributions and must be given when claiming benefits.

family

66 names
67 citizenship
68 parents
69 adoption
70 living together
71 marriage
72 divorce

young citizen's passport

INDIVIDUALS ENGAGING IN SOCIETY

Citizenship Foundation

names

Within six weeks of birth, the birth and name of a child must be registered with the Registrar General of the Register of Births, Deaths and Marriages. The birth may be registered either in the district in which it took place or elsewhere.

The birth can be registered by either parent if they are married, but only by the mother if they are not. If unmarried parents want both their names to appear on their child's birth certificate, then they must both be present when the child is registered. Names can also be registered later.

Changing your name

Under 16

A child's name can be changed with the agreement of both parents, unless the child is in care or a ward of court. In this case the child's name cannot be changed without the agreement of the court or everyone with responsibility for the child. The child can also object by applying to court.

If a parent wants to change their child's name, but the other parent or the child objects – then the parent or the child can apply for a court order to prevent this. Courts are very reluctant to agree to change a child's name against their wish because of the importance of a name to a child's sense of identity.

In Scotland there is no specific procedure, such as deed poll, to change your name. If you are over 16 you can have a solicitor prepare a statutory declaration, in which you swear in front of the solicitor that, in future, you will be known by another name. Alternatively, if you can produce evidence to the Registrar General that you have been using your new name for two years, he or she may change your birth certificate to show this. However, changing your name can cause problems, and should only be done for a very good reason.

Over 18

You can call yourself what you like and, if you want to change your name, you can just go ahead and do it. If you are married, you will usually need the agreement of your spouse. But you can't change your name to mislead or defraud someone.

Although you are free to be known by whatever name you wish, it can be difficult to prove your identity if the name you use is not the same as the one on your birth certificate. The best way to confirm your new name is by a applying to the Registrar General of the Register of Births, Deaths and Marriages who will record this provided the name has been used for a period of two years. Your local Citizens' Advice Bureau or a solicitor can give you more information on this.

If you marry

Women have the right to change their surname when they marry – but they don't have to. A woman can keep her own family name, or make a new one by joining her name with that of her husband. A new surname becomes official by signing the marriage register, then registering with the Registrar General of the Register of Births, Deaths and Marriages.

A man can also change his name to that of his wife upon marriage.

CITIZENSHIP

Most of our legal rights and responsibilities arise just because we are living, working, studying etc in a particular place – in our case, Britain. This is citizenship in its widest sense.

Sometimes, however, people need to know which country they are legally connected to (or what their nationality is). Countries can base their rules on a number of questions, such as where the person was born, how long they have lived in the country and where their parents were born or live.

In brief Anyone born in the United Kingdom before 1st January 1983 is automatically a British citizen. If you were born in the UK on or after this date, you are a British citizen by birth if either of your parents are British citizens or they are entitled to live here permanently. If your parents are not married, only your mother's position counts.

Becoming a British citizen by naturalisation or registration depends on a number of different factors, such as if you marry a British citizen, how long you have lived here, if you are permanently settled here (or intend to remain here permanently) and if you are of 'good character'.

This is a complicated process and you will need specialist advice. Your local Citizens' Advice Bureau can help you find this.

parents

There are no laws that list the exact rights and duties of parents. It is impossible to write down everything a parent should do for a child.

Instead, the law states that all married parents and unmarried mothers automatically have parental responsibility for their children. An unmarried father does not have automatic parental responsibility for his child. He can obtain parental responsibility by signing the birth register jointly with the mother, by agreement with her, by marrying her, or by being granted parental responsibility by the courts.

Parental responsibility This means having the responsibility and authority to care for the child's physical, moral, and emotional needs.

When a child or young person is taken into care, parental responsibility is given to the local authority, although parents do keep certain rights and responsibilities.

The law puts the interest of the child first. The powers that parents have to control their children are for the benefit of the child, not the parent. Those who deal with children in a legal setting, such as social workers, doctors and lawyers, must take careful note of what a child says, particularly when the child is able to understand all the issues involved. Parental responsibility ends when the child reaches 16, although a parent remains responsible for providing direction and guidance until the child is 18. A parent's duty to provide financial support for a child continues beyond the age of 16 if the child is in full-time education or training.

Providing a home Parents have a duty to look after and care for their children until they are 16. However, once someone reaches the age of 16 they can normally leave home without their parent's permission. The police and other authorities are unlikely to stop anyone leaving home, even against their parent's wishes, unless they are under 16, in some kind of danger, or are unable to look after themselves. See **home**, page 77.

Discipline Parents have the right and duty to discipline their child – and this can include smacking. But corporal punishment must be "moderate and reasonable". If it is too harsh the parents risk prosecution or having their child's name put on the child protection register or the child being taken into care. In several other European countries, it is illegal for a parent to strike a child and this is being considered in Scotland.

Education Parents have a duty to make sure that their child has a suitable full-time education, between the ages of 5–16. See **education**, page 26.

use the law with care try talking first

BABY-SITTING

Religion

Parents can decide the religion (if any) in which their child will be brought up. If they can't agree between themselves, they can go to court, where a judge will decide what is in the best interests of the child.

A court will listen to the views of the child concerned and these will be respected if the child clearly understands what is involved.

Medical treatment

In practice young people, aged 16 and over, can almost always agree to their own medical treatment without referring to their parents. Before treating a young person under 16, however, a doctor will normally try to obtain the parent's permission unless it is an emergency or the young person is clearly able to understand what the treatment involves.

There is no law giving the minimum age for a baby-sitter, nor one stating how old a child must be before it can be left alone. Parents must take all the circumstances into account. For example, the age of the baby-sitter, the availability of the parent(s) and the health of the children being looked after, count as relevant factors.

Parents have a legal duty to care for their children; some of that responsibility is temporarily passed on to a baby-sitter when the children are in their care. This means that parents must choose a baby-sitter who is able to look after their children properly. If a serious accident occurs while they are out, the parents may have to convince a court that they had done all that they could to make sure their child was being looked after properly. A baby-sitter under 16 will probably be thought too young to deal with an emergency.

adoption

Anyone who is under 18, and has never been married, can be adopted. A couple or an individual wishing to adopt a child must usually be at least 21. If a married couple wish to adopt, and one partner is the father or mother of the child, they need only be 18.

When children are adopted, they are treated in law almost as if they had been born to the couple or person who adopted them. Parents who adopt children are advised to be open about their child's birth family from the start.

At 18, people who have been adopted have the right to see a copy of their original birth records, and can get more information from the agency that arranged their adoption. An interview with a counsellor to prepare them for this is available.

Further help for adopted people and their birth relatives who wish to get in touch is available through the Adoption Contact Register and NORCAP. See life, page 15, and contacts.

living together

An increasing number of couples live together, sometimes with the thought of getting married later on, and sometimes not. Although this is a matter of personal choice, the law treats married and unmarried couples very differently.

Money and finance

A couple who live together without getting married are under no duty to look after one another, or to provide each other with financial support, unless it is something they have specifically agreed to do.

When children are involved, both parents, whether married or unmarried, have a legal responsibility to look after them and provide for them until they reach the age of 16, or even later if they remain in full-time education.

If a married person dies without making a will, their partner is entitled to all or most of their possessions. But if they were not married, it can be very difficult for the partner to obtain any of the deceased's possessions.

Children

Parents who are married share parental responsibility for their children. This means that both can make decisions about their children's upbringing. Unmarried fathers have this right if the couple have signed a parental responsibility agreement, or if the father has made a successful application to court for parental responsibility.

Home

A married couple have equal rights to occupy their home, whether they rent or own it. This continues even if their marriage fails, unless the court orders otherwise.

Unmarried couples do not have this right. If the home is in just one person's name, the non-owner may not have any right to occupy the property. However, non-owners may possibly obtain rights over the house if they make mortgage payments or improvements to the structure of the property. Couples can avoid difficulties caused by this by using a solicitor to write a formal contract setting out what would happen to their house and contents etc. should the relationship come to an end.

Breaking up Unlike a married couple, people who live together can end their relationship anytime they choose, without having to go to court.

use the law with care **try talking first**

Getting married

Legally, no one can be forced to marry against their wishes, and each partner must be 16 or over and unmarried. Marriages involving someone aged 15 or under, or members of the same sex (even after a sex change operation), are not recognised in law.

In Scotland, under the *Marriages (Scotland) Act 1977*, you must obtain a marriage schedule from the District Registrar in the district where you live. You can then be married in a religious ceremony provided it is a religion authorised under the *Marriages (Scotland) Act 1977* or you can marry in a civil ceremony at a registration office.

Being married to more than one person at the same time – called bigamy – is normally a crime. But the marriages are recognised in Scotland if they took place in a country that allows marriages of this kind, and if each partner was legally free to marry in that way.

Civil partnerships

The *Civil Partnership Act 2004* allows same-sex couples, aged 16 and over, to register their partnership in a similar way to a civil marriage, and gives same-sex couples the same legal rights as people who marry. The law took effect from 5th December 2005 in Scotland and means that, for the first time, same-sex couples have the same rights to property, benefits, inheritance and parental repsonsibility as those who are married.

The ceremony can take place in a registry office (or other premises with an appropriate licence) – but not in a church or other religious building. There are indications, however, that some local authorities are reluctant to allow civil partnership ceremonies to take place on council property.

If either or both partners wish to end the partnership, a formal court process takes place, through which it becomes dissolved.

Engagement

Until 1970 an engagement was seen as a legal contract. If someone breaks off their engagement today there is usually not even a duty to return the engagement ring. The ring is seen as a gift, and may be kept, unless it was originally agreed to return it if the marriage did not take place.

VIOLENCE

A court can make an order, called an interdict, to protect a victim of domestic violence and can order one partner to leave the home for the other's protection – even if they are married. It is important for anyone in this situation to get advice from a solicitor as soon as possible.

divorce

A couple who no longer wish to live together, can either end their marriage by divorce, or separate, keeping the marriage legally alive. A separation may simply mean living apart, or it can be made more formal through a court order.

When one or both partners decide to divorce, an application is made to the local sheriff court or the Court of Session. It is usually made through a solicitor, but can be done by one of the partners alone. There is no requirement in Scotland that the couple have to be married for 12 months before the divorce can begin.

If both partners can agree over their finances and together make satisfactory plans for the care of their children, it will probably not be necessary for either to appear in court. Nor will there be any publicity in the papers. There are thousands of divorces each year, and the press cannot report the case unless the divorce is contested or reporting restrictions are lifted.

When the Judge is satisfied that the appropriate arrangements have been made, that all the information is correct and that the marriage has broken down and cannot be saved, he or she will grant a decree of divorce. When this is granted, the marriage comes to an end.

Grounds for divorce

A person who applies for a divorce must prove to the court that their marriage has irretrievably broken down and that one of the following five things has happened:

1. the other partner has committed adultery, i.e. had sexual intercourse with another man or woman and it is intolerable to live together,

2. the other partner has behaved unreasonably. This covers many things, including assault, refusing to have children, being excessively dirty or anti-social,

3. they have lived apart for two years, and they both want a divorce,

4. they have lived apart for five years and only one partner wants a divorce,

5. or one partner has deserted the other for at least two years immediately before the application.

Children

Parents going through a divorce are encouraged to reach an agreement between themselves over where their children will live and how often they will see each parent. But the judge will accept these arrangements only if satisfied that they are in the best interests of the child. If the child is felt to be old enough to have a view of their own, the judge will talk to them in private.

Parents who cannot agree over this are often advised not to go straight to court (expensive and stressful for all concerned), but to use independent counsellors to help them sort out their problems. A court will, however, have to approve the final arrangements over children and money. It's usually felt to be in the children's interest to keep in touch with their family, so a judge will rarely stop a parent from seeing a child.

After the divorce, both parents normally keep parental responsibility for their child, and both should consult each other over decisions that affect their child's life, such as education, medical treatment, and religious upbringing.

Step-parents

Step-parents do not have parental responsibility for their stepchildren, but the courts can require them to support a step-child. With their new partner, the step-parent may help with day-to-day things affecting the child, but major decisions should be taken by the child's birth mother and father – or only the mother, if they were not married (unless the father has parental responsibility). To change this, a step-parent may apply for parental responsibility or, together with the birthparent, to adopt the child. See **contacts** for organisations able to give more information about this. If their relationship with the natural parent breaks down, the step-parent will have no rights over the child.

Grandparents

When a marriage ends, it may mean that a child is prevented from seeing other family members, such as grandparents, adding to the child's loss. In this situation, grandparents can apply to a court for permission to carry on seeing the child or to have the child stay with them – although this is more difficult to obtain than for parents.

Family disputes

Sometimes parents become involved in legal disputes which directly affect their children – especially if they are getting divorced and cannot agree who the children should live with. In really important cases a young person who shows enough understanding of the issues, can act on their own initiative to instruct a solicitor and even make an application to the court. It is usually much better if their views can be reflected through a counsellor or mediator as the whole process can be very stressful and damaging to relationships with parents or other family members. It is important to get specialist advice, see **contacts**.

home

76 a place of your own
78 tenancies
82 homelessness

young citizen's **passport**

INDIVIDUALS ENGAGING IN SOCIETY

Citizenship Foundation

a place of your own

Where do I look?

Advertisements for accommodation are found in local newspapers, supermarkets and the student union, if you are at college. The local council housing department can tell you whether you are likely to qualify for council housing, and can also give you details of local housing associations.

You can also try solicitors' offices, estate agents and accommodation agencies. These agencies are not allowed, by law, to charge you for information about housing or lists of vacancies. Don't agree to pay them a fee. Normally they are paid for their services by the landlord. If you are asked for money and have any doubts, check first with the local Citizens' Advice Bureau or Shelterline, see **contacts**. Don't be rushed. It's a good idea to get someone to look at the place with you.

You can own a house if you are over 16 but standard practice with banks and building societies is not to grant mortgages if you are under eighteen and you may find it difficult to take on a private tenancy if you are under 18.

What's the rent? What does it include – council tax, electricity, service charges etc? How often is it paid, and who is it paid to? Is any rent payable in advance? Rent paid in advance will be lost if you leave without giving the right amount of notice.

Your rent is fixed at whatever rate you agreed with your landlord. If you think the rent demanded is too high you can ask the Rent Assessment Committee to decide what is reasonable for the property (ring your local council, or see under 'rent officer' in the phone book). If you are a short assured tenant (most are), you must do this within the first six months of the tenancy. There is no charge for this, but the committee can assess your rent only if there are enough similar flats or houses being let in the area.

The rate fixed by the rent assessment committee applies for at least 12 months from the date the rent was fixed, and a tenant can make only one application to the

HOUSING BENEFIT

If you are on a training programme, Income Support or a low wage, you may qualify for Housing Benefit from your local council. Your local housing advice centre or Citizens' Advice Bureau can help you work out what you're entitled to. Housing Benefit is not available to full-time students, unless they have children or have a disability.

Discrimination

A landlord must not discriminate against a would-be tenant on grounds of race or sex, unless the property is being shared with others, and the landlord (or close relatives) live at the property. It is also against the law for someone who sells or lets property to discriminate against a disabled person. Landlords and members of their immediate family who let out rooms to less than seven people (or two other households) in their own homes are not affected.

use the law with care try talking first

committee. It's a good idea to take advice before you do this, as your landlord may try to evict you. Sometimes the committee can put the rent up as well as down.

Do I pay a deposit? This is an amount (often equal to a month's rent) paid to the landlord, or the agent, at the start of the tenancy. Always ask for a receipt when you hand over your deposit.
If you cause damage or leave bills or rent unpaid, the landlord can take what you owe from your deposit. Try to agree any deductions with the landlord before you leave, otherwise you may find you've lost more of your deposit than you should.

Is there a service charge? This is money paid to look after the building and clean those parts that are shared, such as the stairs and corridors in a block of flats. Check what is covered by this figure and decide whether it seems reasonable. If you rent your home from a private landlord or a housing association and pay a variable service charge as well as rent, you have the right to ask the landlord exactly how the service charge is calculated.

Do I need references? If so, choose people who have known you for a reasonable length of time, but preferably not a close relative. It is important to ask the person concerned first.

How safe? If possible, check any fire escape, plumbing, electrical fittings, and heating appliances. Landlords must, by law, have all gas appliances checked each year and must get a certificate of safety that you are entitled to see.

Leaving home

If you are 16 or 17 and homeless, or feel that you can no longer live at home because you are being hurt, or because life at home is so bad, you can get help from social services. Under the *Housing (Scotland) Act 1987*, local authorities must provide accommodation for homeless 16 and 17 year olds who are in need or whose welfare would be endangered if accommodation were not provided. However, some local authorities find it difficult to get hold of suitable accommodation for young people, and Income Support is not available to all 16 or 17 year olds.

Therefore, if you can, get advice from a housing advice centre, Citizens' Advice Bureau, or your local council before you do anything.

In care If you are leaving care, your local social services have a legal duty to provide help and advice.

tenancies

If you rent a house from a local authority or housing association landlord you will probably have a Scottish secure tenancy. If you are renting from a private landlord your tenancy will most likely be a short assured tenancy.

Scottish secure tenancies

Under this arrangement, you are entitled to stay in the property generally for as long as you wish, as long as you keep to the terms of your tenancy. If you don't, your landlord can obtain a court order to evict you. Otherwise, you will only be required to leave in quite unusual circumstances, for example if the house had to be demolished, in which case the landlord would be expected to find you suitable alternative accommodation.

Short assured tenancies

If you are renting from a private landlord, you will probably have a short assured tenancy, which is normally for a minimum of six months or one year, but can be longer. Once your tenancy has come to an end, the landlord is entitled to try to have you evicted as long as he or she has gone through the correct procedures at the beginning and end of the tenancy.

Remember With any type of tenancy agreement, a number of points should be borne in mind:

- If you're a tenant of a council or a housing association, you will probably have a right to stay in the house as long as you want, provided you keep to the terms of your tenancy. If you are with a private landlord, your rights will be more restricted.
- It is generally a criminal offence for a landlord to evict a tenant without obtaining a court order. If this occurs, the tenant is also normally entitled to damages.
- If your landlord wishes to evict you because you have fallen behind with the rent, generally a court still has to be satisfied that it is reasonable to do so. However, if you are a tenant with a private sector landlord and still owe more than three months' rent at the time of the hearing, the court will generally have to grant an eviction order.
- You cannot leave before the end of your tenancy without giving the notice required in your agreement. If you do, you will be required to pay the balance of your rent, unless there is a clause in your tenancy allowing you to leave by giving an agreed period of notice. You can ask for this to be included in your agreement. This does not normally apply to Scottish secure tenancy agreements,

use the law with care **try talking first**

SUMMARY

If you're a tenant of a council or a housing association, you will probably have a right to stay in the house as long as you want provided you keep to the terms of your tenancy. If, however, you are with a private landlord your rights will be more restricted. It is a complicated area of law and in the event there is any attempt to get you to leave you should take advice since often what may seem a hopeless situation can be resolved in such a way as to allow you to stay or at least give you a reasonable time before you have to leave.

which generally require only one month's notice.

- You have a right to receive from your landlord a written statement of the terms of your tenancy. This includes the date that the tenancy began, the date that it ends, the amount of rent payable, and the date that it is due.

- Your landlord must give you formal notice to leave before taking any court action. If you are in this position it is always a good idea to take advice from a housing advice centre, Shelter (see contacts) or a housing lawyer.

- If no action is taken by either side to end the tenancy, it will continue after the termination date set out on the lease. The amount of time that this will be for generally depends on what is stated in the agreement.

- If you take the joint tenancy of a property with someone else, you are both responsible for making sure that you keep to the terms of the agreement. If one of you leaves before the end of the tenancy, the other becomes responsible for the full rent.

Lodging and hostels

You do not have the same rights if you are in lodgings or if your landlord lives with you in the same house and shares the basic services with you. Your landlady or landlord only needs to give you "reasonable notice" and may not need to apply to a court to have you evicted.

If you are in hostel accommodation with a local council or housing association, they will not generally need a court order to evict you. They can give you notice at any time, as long as they keep to the terms of the hostel agreement.

Council tenants

You have certain rights as a council tenant, which include staying in your house for as long as you want (assuming you pay your rent and do what your tenancy agreement says), taking in lodgers, and being consulted about the running of the estate. The council has a right to take action against tenants who cause a nuisance to others on the estate. In serious cases this has led to tenants losing their homes.

Repairs and maintenance

Who is responsible?

Your landlord is responsible by law for looking after the structure of the building, including outside fittings (such as gutters) and essential services (heating appliances – not cookers – sinks, baths and toilets and the water, gas and electricity supplies). The landlord is also usually responsible for any other repairs that are necessary to keep the house in a habitable condition. Tenants are responsible for repairs for damage that they or their visitors cause, but not for fair "wear and tear". Repairs have to be done within a reasonable period.

> Dear Landlord
> As I told you by (phone/letter) on (date), the water heater at (the address) is broken, and it is your responsibility to put this right under our tenancy agreement. Since this has not been done, I have got (three) estimates for repairs from (names and addresses of firms) which I enclose. Unless I hear from you by (date) that you will do these repairs straightaway, I will have no option but to ask (name your choice) to do the repair. I shall then deduct their bill from future rental payments.
> Yours sincerely,

Getting them done

Tell the landlord when the repairs need doing – and keep paying the rent. If the landlord does nothing and the problem concerns serious questions of health and safety, you can get in touch with the local environmental health office. They have the powers to get something done, and can make the landlord carry out the necessary work. Their number is in the phone book under the name of your local council.

If the problem is less serious, or the environmental health department won't take action, and if you are sure that the landlord is responsible for doing the repairs and has failed to do them within a reasonable period, you can write to the landlord explaining you intend to undertake the work yourself unless he does the repairs, and send at least three estimates of the cost. Give your landlord some time to consider the letter. If the landlord still does not do the repairs you may go ahead with them yourself, taking the cost from your rent. Keep detailed records of everything you've done and a copy of every letter you write and receive. From April 2007, if you have asked for the repairs to be done in writing, and the landlord has not done them, you can complain to the Private Rented Housing Panel. If you are in any doubt, at any stage, seek advice.

Eviction

Generally speaking, you cannot be made to leave the house or flat that you are renting, unless the landlord has given you notice in the correct way and obtained a possession order from a court. In most cases, it is a criminal offence for anyone to evict you without a court order, or to try to force you out with threats. A court order may not be necessary, however, if you live in lodgings or your landlord lives on the premises, but take advice. But your landlord still can't use violence to force you to leave. This is a criminal offence.

If you're threatened with eviction, get advice straightaway from a solicitor or your local council housing department or Citizens' Advice Bureau. Make sure you keep on paying the rent. Failure to pay will make it easier for the landlord to require you to leave.

use the law with care try talking first

Harrassment If your landlord stops short of physical violence, but still behaves in a way designed to make you leave – like changing the locks, shouting abuse or playing loud music – they will be breaking the *Rent (Scotland) Act 1984* and *Housing Scotland Act 1987*. Again your local council, housing advice centre or Citizens' Advice Bureau can help. If physical violence is used or threatened, call the police.

BRIEF CASE: Laurie

A few weeks after signing a six-month tenancy agreement for a bed-sit, Laurie was told to leave. His landlord had decided to sell the house and knew he would get more money for it with Laurie out of his room. The lock on Laurie's door was taken off, and the landlord threatened to tip his possessions into a black plastic bag. Without a job, Laurie spent more than two months sleeping in his car. With legal advice, and using legal aid, he took his case to court. The judge decided Laurie had been illegally evicted and ordered the landlord to pay him £36,500 in compensation – the extra amount of money the landlord made by selling his house without a tenant.

Insurance If you are living in rented accommodation, insurance for the building is normally arranged by the owner. Building insurance will not cover the cost of replacing your things if they are damaged or stolen. You can arrange to insure your belongings through an insurance company or a broker, see money, pages 62–63.

If you have anything valuable, like a camera, stereo or jewellery, you will need to list it separately on the insurance and find out exactly how much it costs to replace. The same applies to something like a bike that may be stolen or lost outside the home.

Some policies will give you the full replacement cost; others take into account wear and tear, and pay you less. If you are under-insured it means that your belongings are insured for less than their real value. If the insurance company discovers this when you make a claim, the amount they pay out is likely to be reduced.

Noisy neighbours The best way to tackle a problem of noise, or any other nuisance, is to talk to the person concerned, if possible, before the situation gets out of hand. Sometimes this is easier and more effective if several people complain together. If this doesn't work, write a simple letter (keep a copy), and allow a reasonable time for your neighbour to respond.

If that fails, get in touch with your local environmental health department. They have powers to investigate and deal with the matter. Usually, they have special teams to deal with anti-social behaviour; powers include ASBOs (anti-social behaviour orders). See also **leisure**, page 90.

homelessness

Council help If you are homeless, the council housing department should be able to help. It has a legal duty to give you advice and help towards finding somewhere to live, but this is not the same as offering you somewhere to stay. The council has to house you only if you are 16 or over and:

- **homeless; and**
- **in priority need; and**
- **have a connection with the local area; and**
- **have not made yourself intentionally homeless.**

You should qualify as a priority need if:

- **you're pregnant; or**
- **you have a child who depends on you; or**
- **you've had to leave your last home because someone was violent towards you; or**
- **you've lost your home through something like a fire or flood; or**
- **your age, health problems or disability makes you vulnerable and unable to cope with being homeless;**
- **you are 16 or 17.**

If you have recently left care you are entitled to suitable accommodation until you are 18. Seek advice from Shelter or other housing advice centres.

Sleeping rough This is dangerous, and places the person at risk of being assaulted. Without an address, it is harder to get a job and even benefit. Someone found sleeping rough or begging more than once may be fined.

SQUATTING

In England and Wales, a squatter is someone who enters and occupies land, or any part of a building, without the owner's permission. Squatting is not a crime, but squatters may commit an offence if they cause damage when getting into the property or to the contents, or by using gas or electricity without first making the proper arrangements.

However, in Scottish Law, there is no equivalent of the so-called "squatters' rights" which exist in England and Wales. In Scotland, occupying a building without permission amounts to trespass, and reasonable force (perhaps involving the police) may be used to effect removal. Often however, a court order is obtained first. That can be done quickly.

leisure

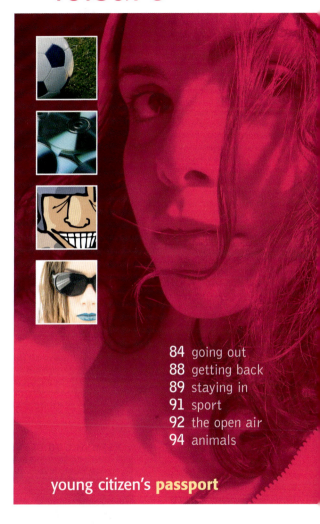

84 going out
88 getting back
89 staying in
91 sport
92 the open air
94 animals

young citizen's **passport**

INDIVIDUALS
ENGAGING IN
SOCIETY

Citizenship Foundation

going out

It may be for fun, but you don't leave your legal rights at home when you go out for the night. If you spend an evening at a match or concert looking at nothing more than a roof support or girder, then you have a right to complain and ask for a refund. It's no excuse for the management to say that you should have arrived earlier for a better seat. Under the law of contract they should have warned you that the view was restricted before selling you the tickets.

There is no simple law setting out people's rights in the event of a change to the advertised programme or the cancellation of a performance. Your legal position will depend on such things as advance publicity, information given when the ticket was sold and the circumstances that forced a change of plan.

Although disgruntled spectators have been successful in taking promoters to court, legal action is not recommended for disappointment over a cancelled event. Some promoters will try to retain goodwill by offering tickets for another performance, or refunds. If they don't, it's worth explaining why you think their action is unreasonable – a key word in cases of this kind.

Hotels, pubs and off-licences The licensing laws controlling the sale of drinks were introduced in the First World War, but have now been substantially changed.

Providing they sell soft drinks and food, pubs can now apply for a children's certificate allowing children under 14, accompanied by an adult, into a bar for the purpose of having a meal. The children, however, have to leave by 8pm.

Once you're 14, it's legal for you to go into the bar of a pub, but only for soft drinks and at the licensee's discretion. At 16, or over, you can buy beer, cider or perry (made from pear juice), to drink with a meal in the dining or restaurant area of a pub. You may find however that the barman exercises his legal discretion not to serve you.

Only when you're 18 can you buy alcohol or drink alcohol in a bar. Drinks with 0.5% or less of alcohol, such as some canned shandy and low alcohol beers, are treated as non-alcoholic. It is an offence to sell alcohol to anyone under 18 – unless it can be shown that the landlord did their best to check the person was 18 or over. It's also an offence for you to buy, or try to buy, alcohol if you are under 18, or to buy or try to buy it for someone under 18. The maximum fine for this is £1,000, and licensees stand to lose their licence after more than one conviction.

The measures of alcohol that you can be sold are legally controlled. A reasonable head forms part of a pint of beer unless the glass has a line measure. The prices of drinks and food should be displayed by law, and should be clearly visible from where the drinks are served.

REFUSING TO SERVE

Pubs and off-licences should refuse to serve anyone with drink who looks as if they've had enough already or if they believe them to be underaged, otherwise they can be charged and fined. Licensees have the right to ban or refuse to serve anyone they choose – unless it is because of their sex, religion, ethnic group or disability.

use the law with care try talking first

Not in public If a young person under 18 is in a public place (e.g. the street), or a place they have entered illegally, and have been drinking, or are about to drink, the police or another accredited person can, under the *Confiscation of Alcohol (Young Persons) Act 1997*, require them to stop drinking and can take away the alcohol. Refusal may lead to arrest or a fine of up to £500.

They can also take alcohol from someone over 18 who is in a public place, if they believe it will be passed to under-age drinkers.

The police can ask for the name and address of anyone from whom they have taken alcohol in these circumstances, and it is an offence to refuse to give these details or to give a false name and address.

In some parts of the country, it is against the law for anyone to drink alcohol on the street or in other public places.

Proof of age If you have trouble proving you are over 18, you can apply for a proof of age card, carrying your name, photograph, date of birth and signature. The largest scheme is run by the Portman Group – an organisation sponsored by Britain's major drinks companies – and a card costs £5. Application forms are available online or from pubs, off-licences and supermarkets, see **contacts**.

Eating out

Quality Whether you're in an expensive restaurant or an ordinary takeaway you have the right to reject any food of a quality below the standard that you are reasonably entitled to expect. What is 'reasonable' depends on such things as the price charged, what the menu says, and basic standards. The laws applying to faulty goods or services also apply. See **money**, pages 51–55.

Complaints It's advisable to complain as soon as you know there's a problem and before eating food you believe is unsatisfactory. The more you are paying the higher the standard you're entitled to expect.

If the quality of your meal is poor or the service is bad, you are entitled to make a reasonable deduction from the bill, but don't leave without paying. Explain to the manager why you are not satisfied, and leave your name and address. It is then up to the restaurant to take this up with you later on if they wish.

Price All restaurants, pubs and cafés must, by law, clearly display the price of food and drink where it is served, so you can read it – usually on a menu, blackboard or notice before you order or sit down at a table.

Service charge A service charge may sometimes be added to the bill in a restaurant. It is usually around ten per cent. If it was made clear before you ordered that service will be included, then you have to pay it. If the service was unsatisfactory, see the manager to ask for a discount. If there is no service charge included, it is up to you whether to leave a tip.

Safety Under the *Food Safety Act 1990*, it is an offence for a restaurant to serve food that is unfit for human consumption. If you are concerned about the hygiene in a place where you have eaten, you can contact your local environmental health office, which has the power to investigate.

Raves

Anyone who organises a rave may need an entertainment licence. To get one the event must meet certain safety standards. Many raves are legal and are arranged in conjunction with the local licensing authorities. Unlicensed raves are illegal.

Under the *Criminal Justice and Public Order Act 1994*, the police have the power to break up an unlicensed open air rave of more than 100 people if the noise and disturbance are likely to cause distress to local people. Under the direction of a senior police officer, the police can order off the land anyone who is preparing, waiting for, or attending the rave. They can also seize and confiscate any sound equipment. Anyone who goes back onto the land within seven days can be fined or imprisoned for up to three months. The police can also stop anyone within five miles of the rave, and order them not to proceed to the gathering. Anyone who refuses to turn back may be fined.

Although the police have the powers to close raves and unlicensed parties that break the law, many forces prefer to get involved only if there is a danger to people's safety or a serious nuisance.

Drugs

Despite the drug culture that surrounds raves the possession of drugs remains illegal and can lead to a criminal record, a fine and imprisonment. In addition, taking Ecstasy causes a rise in body temperature. Coupled with the heat inside the building, there is a serious danger of dehydration or heatstroke if body fluid is not replaced. It's advisable to drink about a pint of water every hour and to take regular breaks. Alcohol doesn't help, as it dehydrates the body even further. For more information on drugs and the law, see **life**, pages 9–12.

GAMBLING

Anyone under 18 is forbidden from going into a casino, betting shop, private club, or into an amusement arcade with gaming machines offering all cash prizes of £10 or more.

Lottery tickets or scratch cards should not be sold to anyone under 16 and winnings cannot be collected by someone below this age.

If you're under 18, you are only allowed into a licensed bingo club if you don't take part.

Gambling contracts can be enforced in law. If the loser fails to pay, he or she can be taken to court – although the *Gambling Act 2005* will change this when it is brought into force in September 2007. If you bet, it's wise to use a reputable bookie.

Nightclubs

Nightclubs must have special licences for entertainment and the sale of alcohol. Like pubs, it's illegal to sell alcohol to someone under 18 or to drunk persons, and owners are within their rights to choose who they will or will not allow in, as long as they do not break the anti – discrimination laws. Clubs who charge lower entry fees for women than men are breaking the law.

The door

Bouncers have no special legal powers. The same laws apply to them as everyone else, which means that they can only use a reasonable amount of force to throw someone out. In certain circumstances this means no force at all – and a bouncer who uses too much force without good reason commits an offence.

Under the *Private Security Industry Act 2001*, all door supervisors must now be licensed. It is an offence for a supervisor or security guard to operate without one.

getting back

If you want to get home safely use a licensed taxi or private hire car or the bus.

Black cabs, licensed taxis

These are under tight licensing control. The vehicles must be checked regularly, the fares are set by law and the drivers may have had to sit an exam to get their licence. Black cabs can be flagged down, as well as hired from a taxi rank. From a rank a taxi driver cannot unreasonably refuse to take a fare. It is a criminal offence for a driver of a cab to lengthen the journey in time or distance without cause.

Under the *Disability Discrimination Act 1995*, newly licensed taxis in most areas have to be fully accessible to disabled travellers. Black cab and licensed taxi drivers are also required to help disabled people in and out of taxis and to help with their luggage – although drivers can claim exemption from these regulations if they have a back injury that prevents them from lifting heavy objects.

Private hire cars

All minicabs, private hire cars and their drivers must be licensed by the local authority. If you want a private hire car, you should either book it in advance or wait in the cab office. Even if there's a meter, it's a good idea to get an estimate of the fare before you set off. If there's not, always agree the fare in advance. Minicabs and private hire cars are generally unaffected by the *Disability Discrimination Act*.

Unlicensed taxis and private hire cars

Unlike black cabs or licensed taxis, these vehicles will not have been specially examined and may not even have a current MOT. They will not be insured to carry fare paying passengers. So passengers have little protection if anything goes wrong.

No entry

The driver of a licensed taxi or hire car who without good reason refuses to take a passenger (including a disabled person) may be prosecuted and fined. Anyone who feels that they are a victim of this, and wishes to do something about it, should make a note of the plate or registration number of the taxi or hire vehicle and report it to their local licensing authority. (The main local council switchboard can provide the number.) The licensing authority will investigate the case and then prosecute the driver if they feel there is sufficient evidence.

use the law with care try talking first

Parties

Drink and drugs

Although you can't buy alcohol from an off-licence until you're 18, anyone over five can drink alcohol on private premises. It is an offence to give alcohol to a child under five, unless given by a doctor or in an emergency.

An offence is committed, under the *Misuse of Drugs Act 1971*, if you knowingly allow anyone into your flat or house to supply an illegal drug to someone else, or allow the smoking of cannabis. Even if you are not taking the drug yourself, you can still be charged, as it is your place they are using. The penalty for someone allowing their flat or house to be used for drug-taking is up to 14 years in prison for a Class A or B drug, or five years for a Class C drug. For more on the law and drugs, see **life** pages 9–12.

Safety

You invite some friends around for the evening and one of them falls down the stairs. If the cause of the accident was the state of the carpet rather than too much beer, you or your parents could be liable for their injuries. This doesn't mean wrapping every sharp corner in cotton wool, but something like a loose piece of stair carpet definitely should be fixed, since it is reasonable for visitors to expect to walk down the stairs safely. You're not expected to guard against the unforeseeable. If someone slides down the banisters and breaks a leg, then that's their problem.

Insurance

If someone is injured in your home you could be required to pay them compensation – although this can be paid through an insurance policy, if you have one. Most householders' insurance policies cover owners for injuries to other people called "third parties" caused by the state of the buildings or its fittings. If you're in rented accommodation, your landlord could be liable – and again it is his or her insurance company that would pay damages. If you face this problem you can check with a solicitor or Citizens' Advice Bureau.

Gatecrashing

Gatecrashing is trespass. The law says that you can use reasonable force to get gatecrashers to leave, but don't start waving a broken bottle around. This is unreasonable and will leave you in more trouble than them.

staying in

Noise If there is a noisy party and the police are called, they can ask people to be quiet, but there's not much else they can do unless they fear there's going to be a breach of the peace – that is some kind of disorder. Then arrests will almost certainly be made.

However, if you are being disturbed by noise from a neighbour between 11pm and 7am, you can ring the local environmental health department, which must investigate your complaint as soon as possible. Under the *Environmental Protection Act 1990*, they have the power to send an officer to the house to measure the noise and decide whether it is excessive. If it is, the person believed to be responsible will be given a warning notice, requiring the noise to be switched off or turned down within ten minutes. An offence is committed if the noise continues, the officer can decide to prosecute or issue an on the spot fine of £100. If an on the spot fine is paid within 14 days no further legal action can be taken for the offence; if it is not paid, a court can impose a higher fine.

If the warning notice is ignored, the officer can also obtain a warrant (often very quickly) to go into the building and remove the sound equipment that is being used.

For other problems with noisy neighbours, see **home**, page 81.

TV, video, music and games A licence is required if anyone in a household uses a TV, video recorder and/or any other television apparatus such as a television enabled computer. One licence covers all the equipment in a single home. If rooms are rented separately, a licence must be obtained for the TV equipment in each room. A licence will also cover a television powered by batteries used by a full-time student living away from home.

Copyright Copyright laws give writers, artists, publishers etc. the right to take action against anyone who makes a copy of, or broadcasts their work without permission. Breaking copyright is not a criminal offence and the law is only usually enforced against people who are making illegal copies in large numbers or to sell.

Books, plays, films and music written or made since 1 August 1989 are protected by copyright law for 70 years after the author's death (50 years if created before then). Computer generated work and broadcasts are covered for 50 years from the time they were made.

You can make a tape of a TV or radio broadcast for your own use, but only so you can view or listen to it at a more convenient time. Strictly speaking, it's against the law to record a programme if you intend to keep it as part of a collection or because you find it particularly interesting or enjoyable. Copying a CD, tape or computer game belonging to someone else is also illegal.

■ BRIEF CASE

The EasyInternetCafé burned CDs of Internet downloads (including MP3 music) on behalf of their customers and for profit. Some of the downloads were Sony's copyright and they successfully sued the Café to stop it being done.

Safety

It's an offence to be drunk at a football or rugby match or to have alcoholic drinks in the ground, and even on a football supporters' coach or train travelling to or from the event.

Risks and the duty of care

Anyone who plays sport must expect to suffer the sorts of injuries normal to the game concerned. But intentional or reckless damage to someone else is another matter, and the player responsible can be sued for damages and prosecuted for a criminal offence. Organisers of sporting events also have a duty to see that players, visitors, spectators and passers-by are reasonably safe.

■ BRIEF CASE: Football

A Stockport County player was awarded £250,000 after his career was ended through injuries suffered in a match against Swansea City. The court decided that he was brought down by a tackle aimed at the legs, rather than the ball, which did not reflect the reasonable care that players should show towards one another.

Banned

Under the *Football (Disorder) Act 2000*, a court can ban a person from attending domestic or international football matches. They can be required to report to a police station before a match and to surrender their passport if banned from an international game.

the open air

All land in the United Kingdom is owned by someone – private landowners, a local authority, government body (e.g. Ministry of Defence), or the Crown, (the Queen). The *Land Reform (Scotland) Act 2003* gives everyone access rights to cross land, or be in or on land, water or air for recreational or educational purposes, providing the right to be on land or water is exercised responsibly. This means that you can, for example, walk, swim or climb anywhere, as long as you do no harm to the landowners' property.

Footpaths

If a route across a piece of land has been used for 20 years or more without interruption, that route may become a right of way. A right of way can be lost through disuse, however, this is less important now the rights of access to the countryside have been established. Strictly speaking, footpaths are for walkers only. It's a criminal offence to drive a motorbike or car on a path, however, some rights of way permit vehicular and other use. Footpaths are shown on Ordnance Survey maps – but if you need to check on a path, you can ask to look at the maps in the local council planning office who may be able to give you information on the particular path, otherwise contact the Scottish Rights of Way and Access Society (Scotways), see **contacts**.

The *Land Reform (Scotland) Act 2003* has dramatically improved access to the countryside in Scotland. Your local authority will take action against any person putting up a misleading sign, such as "private" that discourages people from using a public right of way. If you come across a problem of this kind and want something done, contact the local council.

The local council's Rights of Way Officer has a duty to make sure that public rights of way are kept open and free from obstruction. It's the local council's responsibility to maintain footpaths so that people can walk along them, and the job of the landowner to look after stiles and gates along the path, footpath, or bridleway.

BULLS

Checking your legal rights here needs some farming knowledge and the ability to tell one breed of bull from another without getting too close. All dairy bulls (breeds like Friesian, Guernsey and Jersey) are banned from fields crossed by public paths. Other types of bull are allowed only if they are in with cows or heifers, which apparently makes them much less aggressive.

use the law with care try talking first

Fishing

You can fish in the sea and in tidal waters at any time, unless there are local by-laws forbidding it. All fishing rights in rivers, ponds and lochs in Scotland are owned, which means you need to pay for the permission of the owner to fish. Some local authorities own fishing rights and permit their citizens to fish free or for minimum charge. Contact your local authority leisure service for information.

Pollution

The Scottish Environmental Protection Agency asks members of the public to report any environmental incident – on rivers, lakes, canals, or the coastline – or the dumping of rubbish, by ringing their local Scottish Environmental Protection Agency office (number in the phone book).

Beaches

Land between the low and high tide lines is the property of the Crown – but there is almost never a problem in walking along a beach. The *Land Reform (Scotland) Act 2003* gives powers to the public to access beaches providing they do no harm to the landlord's interests.

BRIEF CASE: Katrina

Katrina noticed that the water in Ackhurst Brook near where she lived was an unusual colour – particularly around the discharge pipe used by a local factory. She rang the Environment Agency who sent an officer to investigate. The officer reported that the water was discoloured and smelt foul and contained pieces of food that looked like shells from baked beans – which is just what they were. The company admitted polluting the river and was fined £5,000.

animals

Wildlife

The *Wildlife and Countryside Act 1981* protects a wide range of wild animals, birds and plants and covers killing, injuring, taking or possessing and disturbing their place of shelter or protection. For an up-to-date list of protected species, see Whitakers Almanack, available in most libraries and on the RSPB website. *The Wild Mammals (Protection) Act 1996* makes it an offence to inflict unnecessary suffering on any wild mammal.

Pets

Under the *Pet Animals Act 1951,* it is an offence to sell a pet animal to anyone below the age of 12. Under the *Protection of Animals (Scotland) Act 1912*, a pet owner has a legal responsibility to care for the animal and make sure it does not suffer unnecessarily. It is an offence to be cruel to the animal or to abandon it if it is likely to cause the animal unnecessary suffering.

Pet owners are also responsible for any damage their animal causes if they knew (or should have known) it was likely to cause such damage, or if their animal is defined as dangerous.

Dangerous animals are known, in law, as those that are not domesticated in this country that might be expected to have dangerous characteristics, such as a monkey or venomous snake. Anyone keeping an animal of this kind must have a licence.

Dogs

Under the *Control of Dogs Order 1992*, anyone owning a dog must make sure that it wears a collar with the name and address of its owner when it is in a public place. If a dog fouls any public place, e.g. a footpath or park, the person in charge of the dog commits an offence if he or she fails to clear up the mess.

It is an offence under the *Dangerous Dogs Act 1991*, to allow a dog to be dangerously out of control in a public place. The owner, or person in charge, of the dog can be fined or imprisoned for up to six months. The court can also order the dog to be destroyed, and can disqualify the owner from keeping a dog in the future. A farmer is allowed to shoot a dog that is not under anyone's control and is worrying livestock on their land.

Under the *Guard Dog Act 1975*, guard dogs should be under the control of a handler or else tied up and prevented from roaming freely. A warning notice should also be displayed. The Act does not apply to dogs guarding private houses or farmland.

BRIEF CASE: Abandoned

One morning, the SSPCA received an anonymous telephone call explaining that a dog had been abandoned in a house in a district just outside Glasgow. An SSPCA officer went to investigate and, with the help of the police, broke into the empty house, where they found a young retriever, with neither food nor water, and in a very distressed condition. The owner was traced and admitted the dog had been left alone for ten days. He was charged and found guilty of cruelty and abandonment, fined £150 and banned from keeping an animal for 10 years.

 CONTACTS see pages 142–149 for organisations able to give help & advice

travel
and transport

96 holidays
98 getting about
100 cars & motorbikes
104 driving
106 accidents

young citizen's **passport**

INDIVIDUALS ENGAGING IN SOCIETY

Citizenship Foundation

holidays

Package holidays

When you book a holiday, you are making a contract with the tour organiser – that is the company responsible for arranging the package. This is usually the tour operator, but it can also be the travel agent, particularly if you have asked for extra arrangements to be made, not included in the brochure.

Although holiday brochures are designed to show the hotel or resort at its best, the *Package Travel, Package Holidays and Package Tours Regulations 1992* state that they must be accurate and not misleading. If the room or the swimming pool that you were promised is not available, you may be able to claim compensation because of the failure of the company arranging the holiday to keep its side of the contract. It is an offence, under the *Trade Descriptions Act 1968*, for a firm to make a statement that it knows to be false about the goods or services it provides. Prosecutions for this are usually made by local trading standards officers.

It's important to tell the travel agent or tour operator if you have any special needs at the time you make the booking.

Before you sign or hand over any money, read the small print and check what it says about changes to your schedule. Under certain circumstances, travel organisers can alter flight times or accommodation arrangements provided they make this clear in the brochure or contract. If you pay all or part of the cost of the holiday by credit card, you may be entitled to claim a full or partial refund from the credit card company if the firm organising the holiday fails to keep its side of the contract. For more information on paying by credit card, see **money** page 58.

BEFORE YOU GO

- **Check whether you need to have any vaccinations, and think about getting medical insurance, see below.**
- **If you are travelling in the European Union, get a European Health Insurance Card by applying online or by filling in a form at a main post office – allowing you free or reduced medical costs – you will receive a card which you should take with you on holiday.**
- **Check your passport is up to date and whether you need a visa for the country you are visiting. Passports are not needed for travel to the Republic of Ireland.**
- **If you're thinking of hitching, check on advisability before you go. In some countries it is illegal.**

If you need to know more about travel requirements or conditions, ring the embassy of the country concerned, or visit the Foreign & Commonwealth Office website at www.fco.gov.uk or telephone their Travel Advice line on 020 7008 0232/0233.

use the law with care try talking first

TRAVEL AND MEDICAL INSURANCE

Travel insurance will protect you from losses while you're away and even illness before you go.

Take the policy with you on holiday, so that if anything goes wrong you can make sure you keep to the terms of the agreement.

If you go abroad, book through a travel company registered with ABTA, IATA or ATOL. If the travel firm belongs to one of these organisations, you'll find their symbol in the brochure. They will cover the cost of getting you home, or compensate you for your losses if the company you've booked with goes bust while you're away, or before you've left.

Passports Everyone who travels abroad, including young children, must have their own passport. However, children already included on someone else's passport before October 1998 can continue to travel abroad with the passport holder until either the child reaches 16, the passport expires or the passport is submitted for amendment.

A passport for someone aged 16 or older costs £42 and is valid for ten years, for travel to any country of the world. A passport for someone under 16 costs £25 and is valid for five years.

If something goes wrong If there is a problem with the holiday that the travel company has provided, tell them or their representative as soon as possible. If you're still not satisfied, make a note of the facts (photographic evidence may be helpful), and then contact the travel firm as soon as you get home.

If you're not satisfied with their reply, write to the managing director of the travel firm. If the company belongs to ABTA, you can have your claim decided by an independent person called an arbitrator. If this is not possible, get advice from the Citizens' Advice Bureau and, if necessary, a solicitor. Going to court is a last resort.

If your luggage doesn't arrive, report the loss immediately. Try to obtain a copy of any reports that you complete. Under international law, the airline is responsible for lost or damaged luggage, but compensation is paid by weight rather than value, and the airline will not be responsible for fragile items. It may be better to claim through your holiday insurance.

If you lose all your cash and your cards, you can go to a bank and arrange for money to be transferred from home. There will probably be a charge, but it should arrive within 24 hours.

If you lose anything valuable, tell the police and get a note from them confirming that you have done this. Contact the travel company if you lose your ticket home, and immediately report the loss of traveller's cheques or credit cards to the company offices. They often let you reverse the charges for the call. It is very important to report losses to your insurance company within the time limit stated in the policy.

If your passport is lost or stolen, contact the British Consulate who have an office in most big cities and should be able to provide you with help or advice.

In trouble Travellers overseas are automatically subject to the laws of the country they are visiting.

If you're arrested insist on the British Consulate being informed. The Consulate will explain the local procedures, including access to a lawyer and the availability of legal aid. A European Union (EU) national can go to any EU Consulate, see **Europe** page 136.

holidays

Taking a car or motorcycle

You'll normally need to get a Green Card from your insurance company, which extends your motor insurance to countries other than Great Britain.

It is also worth checking with a motoring organisation who will advise you whether you need an International Driving Permit (AA, RAC and Green Flag will tell you if you need an IDP and can issue one too).

If you're driving to Spain, you should also take out a Bail Bond (fianza). Under Spanish law, the car and driver can be detained after an accident, but can be released on production of a Bail Bond. The Bond will also help cover the cost of any legal action or fine. Contact your motor insurance company for both the Green Card and Bail Bond.

If you have an accident, tell the police and ask for a record or receipt. It will help with your insurance claim when you get home. For the same reason, it's also a good idea to take notes and photographs of the incident, including pictures of the number plates of the vehicles involved.

Don't sign anything in a language that you don't understand. If you're put under pressure, write "I don't understand" immediately above your signature.

Coming home

If you are returning from a country within the EU, you do not have to pay customs charges on any goods you bought in that country, but nor can you obtain any duty-free concessions. However, there is generally no limit on the amount you can bring in – as long as the goods are for a gift or your own use.

Limits are, however, placed on alcohol and tobacco and anyone who exceeds these must convince the customs that the goods are not going to be sold on. No one under 17 is entitled to a tobacco or alcohol allowance.

Customs officials can check your baggage for prohibited goods or to see if you need to pay any tax or duty if you have been to a country outside the EU. Details of the powers and duties of customs officers are given in the Traveller's Charter, available from libraries and the Customs website: www.hmce.gov.uk/public/travel.

getting about

Buses and trains

Tickets

By the time you're 16, you have to pay full fare on all buses and trains, trams and the Glasgow or London Underground. In some areas full fare is charged on buses from the age of 14.

If you travel on a train or the London Underground without a ticket, you may be charged an on the spot penalty, as well as the cost of your fare. Information about this is displayed in stations where this system is in operation.

If you are stranded at a station without any money for a ticket, your ticket can be bought for you by someone else at another station, with the authorisation sent by telephone to where you are waiting. This is known as a silk arrangement.

Some tickets are cheaper when travelling outside the rush hour, and travel cards give you further reductions.

use the law with care **try talking first**

- A Young Persons Railcard costs £20 (2006 prices) and entitles you to a third off most ticket prices. Everyone aged 16–25 is eligible to have one, as are full-time students aged 26 and over. You can buy the Railcard at large stations, some travel agents and from student services at college or by phone, see contacts.
- An Inter-Rail Pass gives you at least 16 days' rail travel in Continental Europe from £140, with discounts available on Eurostar and many cross Channel ferries. You must be under 26, be a citizen of or have lived in Europe for at least six months and have a passport. Inter-Rail cards are available from selected stations and travel agents.
- Student/Young Persons Coachcards entitle young people aged 16–25, and full-time students aged over 26, to a 30 per cent discount on UK coach journeys. One year cards cost £10, and £25 buys a card valid for three years.
- The Under 26 International Youth Card and the Euro<26 card provide members with discounted air fares worldwide, and also offers reductions on places to stay and visit. See contacts.

COMPLAINTS

If your train (or bus) is late, there's not a lot in law that you can do about it. When you buy a ticket, you have no legal guarantee that the train will run on time (or even at all), or that you'll have a seat when it does come. All this is explained in the small print, known as the conditions of carriage, which can be checked at station ticket offices.

Under the Passengers' Charter you may be offered 20% of the ticket price in compensation if you're stuck on a train that has been seriously delayed, for one hour or more, or if you have a season ticket for a train service that has been below the standard set for punctuality or reliability.

If you have a complaint about a train service, you can ask for a complaints form at a station or write to the customer relations manager for the route you have travelled on.

BRIEF CASE: Emma

Emma bought a ticket for a day trip to Edinburgh, saying that she wanted to travel on the next train, leaving in 15 minutes. When the inspector checked her ticket on the train, she asked Emma to pay a further £6, as she had been undercharged by the booking clerk. Although Emma claimed that it was the train operating company's mistake in selling her the wrong ticket, by law she had to pay the difference. When a contract is made, one side cannot gain by the other side's genuine mistake.

The licence

It is an offence to drive or ride a motor vehicle without the correct licence. You get a full driving licence when you have passed your test, and the licence will be valid until you are 70. Licences for drivers over 70 are issued for three years at a time.

New licences are now the size of a credit card and contain the holder's photograph. Old paper licences will be changed to the new format when they are renewed or if the details need to be changed. You must tell DVLA (see **contacts**) of any change of address immediately – or risk a fine.

If you want to learn to drive, you need a provisional driving licence. Application forms are available from post offices. When you get your licence, sign it immediately – don't drive until you have done so. Car drivers can hold the same provisional licence until they are 70. A motorcyclist's provisional licence is only valid for two years.

Learning to drive a car

When you are driving on a provisional licence you must display 'L' plates, which should be removed or covered up when the vehicle is not being driven by a learner. You must not drive on a motorway, and you must have someone with you in the front passenger seat of the car who is over 21 and has held a full EU driving licence for at least three years. This person must be fit to drive and must not have had more than the legal amount of alcohol.

The driving test is in two parts, a written theory exam and a practical test. The theory paper, which must be passed before taking the practical test, lasts 40 minutes and is made up of 35 multiple-choice questions. Driving test theory

papers are now conducted on computer, with results given within half an hour.

Learning to ride a motorcycle, moped or scooter

Motorcyclists also have to take a theory paper and a practical test to gain a licence, unless they already have a full car licence, when only the practical test is required. Before you can ride a motorcycle on the road, you must successfully complete a Compulsory Basic Training course, unless you had a full car licence on 1st February 2001 and only want to ride a moped (with an engine of up to 50cc and a maximum speed of no more than 30mph).

Motorcyclists must learn on a machine no larger than 125cc. After passing the practical test, they are restricted for two years to bikes with a power output of up to 25 kw or 33 bhp, after which they may ride any size of bike. Riders over the age of 21 who don't want to wait this long to ride a larger bike can choose to take further tests, known as direct and accelerated access, see **contacts**.

Learner motorcyclists may not ride on a motorway, nor carry a pillion passenger, unless the passenger is also licensed to ride that type of machine. Mopeds, scooters, and motorised skateboards cannot be used on the public roads without a licence, road tax and insurance.

use the law with care try talking first

MOT

Most vehicles that are three or more years old must pass an MOT test if they are to be used or left on the road.

Road tax

A car or motorbike must display a current tax disc, whether it is being used or just standing on the road. The fine for breaking this regulation is normally about twice the cost of the disc. The Driving and Vehicle Licensing Agency (usually known as the DVLA), now has powers to wheel clamp and remove vehicles not showing a current disc, and to charge a fee for their release. It is a crime to use a tax disc belonging to another vehicle.

If you have a vehicle that you take off the road (e.g. for repairs) and decide not to tax, you must inform the DVLA on the reminder form sent to you when the vehicle licence is due for renewal. The penalty for not doing this is a fine of up to £1,000.

Insurance

It is an offence to drive, ride or even place a motor vehicle on the road without insurance. The penalties for this are very heavy, and it makes no difference for someone to say it was a genuine mistake and that they thought they were insured. Failure to have insurance means a fine and penalty points on a licence, and possible disqualification.

It is also an offence for someone to allow their car or motorcycle to be used by a person who is not insured to drive it.

There are three different kinds of motor insurance, offering different levels of cover:

- **third party insurance only pays for damage caused to other people or their property (and not to your own vehicle). This is the minimum level of insurance cover required by law;**
- **third party fire and theft gives you further protection by covering your vehicle against theft or fire damage;**
- **fully comprehensive insurance is usually the most expensive, but covers the cost of accident repair damage to your vehicle as well as compensating you and others for injuries or damage in the accident.**

When you apply for any insurance, make sure the information you give is accurate and complete. If it's not, your insurance will be invalid. It's an offence knowingly to make a false statement to obtain insurance. For more information, see **money**, page 62.

■ BRIEF CASE: Sarah

Sarah bought a Morgan sports car, and insured it for her and her fiancé to drive. The car, worth £26,000, was stolen. When she claimed on her insurance, it came to light that her fiancé had received a serious motoring conviction several years ago, which Sarah had failed to mention on the application form. The insurance policy was therefore not valid, and Sarah received no compensation for the loss of her car.

cars & motorbikes

AT WHAT AGE?

At 14 you can ride an electrically powered pedal cycle.

At 16 you can ride a moped up to 50cc, a small tractor, mowing machine or invalid car. If you receive a disability living allowance, at the higher rate, you can also drive a car.

At 17 you can drive a car with up to eight passenger seats, a motor tricycle, a motorbike up to 125cc, a large tractor and a van or lorry up to 3.5 tons.

At 18 you can drive a van or lorry up to 7.5 tons.

At 21 you can drive all other vehicles. For hiring a car, most car hire companies have a minimum age of 21 or 23.

Traffic offences

Every vehicle on the road must meet a whole set of regulations covering brakes, tyres, lights, mirrors, steering and even windscreen washer bottles (which must, by law, never be empty). A police officer may stop a vehicle at any time to check that it is in roadworthy condition, and it is no excuse for the driver to claim that they didn't realise a light wasn't working. These are absolute offences and apply even if the driver was completely unaware of the problem.

If the police believe a vehicle is not roadworthy, they can instruct the driver to get it checked and repaired by a garage (usually within 14 days), give the driver a fixed penalty or call up a specially trained vehicle examiner to inspect the car or bike there and then. A police officer who feels a vehicle is so dangerous that someone will probably be injured if it is used any further, can immediately ban it from being driven.

Cycling

Cyclists are expected to follow the same basic laws as other road users. They have a duty of care to pedestrians, other riders and road users. It is an offence, under the *Highways Act 1835*, to ride a bicycle (or tricycle) on the pavement – a law that applies to riders of all ages. Police officers now have the power to impose a £20 fixed penalty fine on cyclists who ride on the pavement. It is also against the law to wheel a bike past a red traffic light or to ride it across a zebra crossing.

It is an offence to ride under the influence of alcohol or drugs. There is no breath test for cyclists; a court would instead be guided by evidence from the officer who made the arrest.

BUYING A CAR

• A small popular car is usually less of a financial risk. Spare parts are cheaper and easier to obtain, insurance costs lower and it will probably be easier to sell when you want to change it.

• A car bought privately is usually cheaper than one bought from a dealer, but you have fewer rights if things go wrong. The *Sale of Goods Act 1979* (see money, page 51), gives greater protection if you buy from a dealer. A car bought privately need only be "as described". The legal expression "caveat emptor" (meaning "buyer beware"), particularly applies when buying a second-hand car. It is notoriously difficult to get problems sorted out once you have paid for the car.

• Look at the car in daylight. Take someone along with you who knows about cars. Check the owner's purchase documents to see if any hire-purchase payments are still due. For between £100–£300 the RAC, AA or Green Flag will inspect and report on the mechanical state of the car, check on the HP payments and tell you whether the car has been stolen or is an insurance write-off. HPI Autodata or AA Car Data provide a similar service at a slightly lower cost, without the mechanical inspection.

• Look to see if the car's mileage tallies with the MOT certificate and the service history. You can also check with previous owners. Ask the dealer if they have tried to verify the mileage – they have to do this by law. Be wary if there is a sticker on the speedometer indicating that there is no guarantee that the mileage is accurate.

• Ask to see the Vehicle Registration Document (V5). If it's a private sale, it should contain the seller's name and address. It also gives the Vehicle Identification Number (VIN), which should correspond with the number stamped on identification plates under the bonnet and on the floor. If you have any doubts, leave the car alone.

• If you buy a car that turns out to be stolen, it remains the property of the true owner – meaning that you will almost certainly lose your money, unless you can get it back from the person from whom you bought the car.

■ BRIEF CASE: Anna

Anna went to look at a Ford Escort, advertised privately in her local paper. She asked the seller if the car had been in an accident. He said no, but having bought the car, Anna later found evidence of major crash repairs. She went back to the seller, pointed out the car was not as described and eventually got her money back. However, if the car had just been unreliable (even breaking down on her first drive), there is probably little she could have done, as there is nothing in law that states that a car bought privately must be of satisfactory or reasonable quality.

brief case

Safety

Seat belts and crash helmets

Seat belts (front and rear), where fitted, must be worn by drivers and passengers. If a passenger in your car does not wear a belt, it is he or she who will be prosecuted, not you – unless the passenger is under 14, when it is your responsibility. Children under 12 and under four feet five inches (1.35m) tall must sit on a safety seat or booster cushion.

Motorcyclist and pillion passengers must both wear an approved safety helmet on all journeys. This regulation does not apply to a follower of the Sikh religion while he is wearing a turban. Dark visors may not be worn at night or when visibility is poor.

SPEED LIMITS

Cars and motorcycles are limited to
- **30 mph in built-up areas, unless marked otherwise,**
- **60 mph on single carriageways,**
- **70 mph on dual carriageways and motorways.**

Speed limits are lower for buses, lorries, and cars towing caravans.

Speeding

Speeding is an absolute offence, which means that it is no defence to say that it wasn't dangerous or that you didn't realise that you were breaking the speed limit. Nor is there much point in denying that you were travelling at the speed the police say you were, unless you can prove it. You will usually be fined and given penalty points.

If you break the speed limit, or are seen by the police to be driving carelessly or dangerously, you must be warned of the possibility of prosecution at the time of the offence or served with a summons within 14 days of the offence. Otherwise you cannot be convicted, unless an accident occurred at the time or immediately after.

Driving badly

Careless driving is to drive in a way that is not how a careful and reasonable driver would behave. Pulling out from a side road without looking is an example of this.

Dangerous driving is to drive in a way that is dangerous to people or property, such as driving very fast through a built-up area or overtaking on a sharp bend. Dangerous driving and causing death by dangerous driving are very serious offences, which courts will punish with fines, disqualification, and imprisonment. If you face such a charge, get in touch with a solicitor straightaway.

Stolen vehicles

Stealing a vehicle to sell on to someone else is theft. Joy-riding, or taking a car to ride around in and then dumping it, is a different offence known as "taking a vehicle without the owner's consent" or TWOC. Both are punishable by a fine or imprisonment.

Mobile phones

Since December 2003 it has been an offence for drivers to use a hand held mobile phone when driving a vehicle. Motorists can be fined from £30 to £1,000 and collect three penalty points.

use the law with care try talking first

■ BRIEF CASE: Peter

Peter was involved in a crash with a motorcycle. He feared that it was his fault and that he would lose his licence, as he already had a number of penalty points. He persuaded his wife Sophie, who was not in the car at the time, to tell the police that it was she who was driving. A week later they both admitted the deception, but were charged with perverting the course of justice. Peter and Sophie were sentenced to four and two months in prison.

Drinking and driving

Alcohol seriously affects a driver's judgement and reactions. There is no law that limits a driver to a certain number of drinks, such as two pints of beer or one glass of wine, but there is a maximum amount of alcohol that you may have in your body while driving or being in charge of a car. In law, being in charge of a car includes simply sitting in the driving seat of a parked car.

The limits

The amount of alcohol in a person's body can be measured in their breath, blood, or urine. A driver will be found guilty of drink-driving if they have more than 35 micrograms of alcohol in 100 ml of breath, 80 mg of alcohol in 100 ml of blood, or more than 107 mg of alcohol in 100 ml of urine.

Breath tests

The police will carry out a road side breath test to check whether a driver has more than the permitted amount of alcohol in their body. Uniformed police can breathalyse anyone whom they reasonably suspect of driving with excess alcohol, or who is involved in a traffic offence or road accident, however minor, even if there is no suspicion of alcohol. A uniformed police officer is also quite entitled to stop motorists at random in order to see whether there is a reasonable suspicion that they have consumed any alcohol. If there is, the officer can go on to ask the motorist to take a breath test.

If the test is positive or the driver refuses a breath test, the driver will be arrested and taken to a police station for further tests.

No escape

A driver who fails to blow into the device properly, or refuses to take a test, will still end up with a heavy fine and have his or her licence endorsed with three to eleven penalty points. Courts rarely accept that there are special reasons for drivers being over the limit. Disqualification from driving is almost automatic. A drunken driver who causes someone's death may be sent to prison for up to ten years, and will be disqualified from driving for at least two years.

■ BRIEF CASE: Jean

Jean had had too much to drink at a party, she didn't want to stay at the house and decided to sleep it off in the back seat of her car. She was woken by the police, breathalysed and found to be over the limit. Although she said she had no intention of driving she was successfully prosecuted and lost her licence for 18 months.

99% PROOF

driving

Courts deal with most motoring offences through a system of penalty points that are entered on a driver's licence. Anyone receiving twelve or more points within a period of three years will almost always be disqualified from driving for at least six months. Details of the points carried for each offence are given in the Highway Code. Drivers who have six or more penalty points on their licence within two years of their test, go back to being a learner until they pass a further test.

accidents

What to do Accidents happen to the most careful of drivers, often through no fault of their own. If you are involved in an accident, there are certain things that you should and should not do…

- **Stop immediately. Try to stay calm, even if people are yelling and screaming at you.**
- **Check that everyone involved in the accident is OK. If anyone is injured, call an ambulance before you do anything else.**
- **You must give your name and address and details of your vehicle to anyone who has reasonable need to know them. This includes a police officer at the scene of the accident, anyone who is injured, anyone whose property is damaged and the owner of any animal injured or killed. (This applies to horses, cows, sheep, goats and dogs – but not cats.) If someone is injured, you must also produce your insurance certificate to show that you are properly insured. If you can't do this at the time of the accident, then you must give this information to the police as soon as possible, and certainly within 24 hours. If you don't, you will be committing an offence.**
- **Make sure you get the name, address, vehicle registration number and insurance details of the other drivers involved and the name and address of any witness.**
- **Contact your insurance company as soon as possible, and also make a detailed note of everything that happened. This should cover the time of day, weather, light, estimated speeds, position of vehicles before and after the accident, what people said and anything else that you think might be relevant. If you can, take photos before anything is moved, or draw a sketch plan as soon as you feel able to do so.**
- **Don't drive away without stopping. It is a criminal offence.**
- **Be cautious if the other driver suggests not calling the police and offers you cash to cover the damage. You may find that the damage to your vehicle costs a lot more than you are being offered. If you both agree to exchange details without reporting the accident to the police then that is okay, as long as nobody is injured and no property has been damaged.**
- **Don't admit it was your fault. You may find later that the other driver was drunk, driving too fast, or without lights – in which case you might not be to blame at all. If you do admit responsibility, your words may end up by being used against you in court and may affect your insurance claim.**

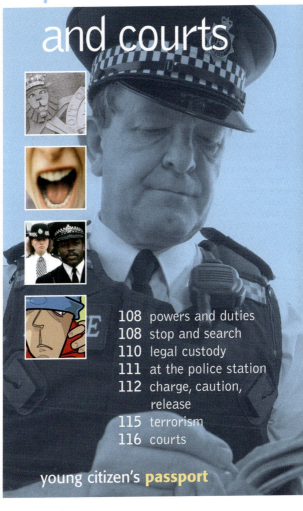

police
and courts

108 powers and duties
108 stop and search
110 legal custody
111 at the police station
112 charge, caution, release
115 terrorism
116 courts

young citizen's **passport**

INDIVIDUALS ENGAGING IN SOCIETY

Citizenship Foundation

powers & duties

Powers and duties

Most of the information that the police receive comes from the general public. Without this help they could do very little.

Much of the law setting out police powers and duties when investigating crime is contained in the *Criminal Procedure (Scotland) Act 1995*. The law sets out rules that the police must follow when searching for and collecting evidence. If they are broken when the police are, say, questioning a suspect, a judge or sheriff may decide that the evidence obtained cannot be used in court, and the police officers concerned may be disciplined.

POLICE DISCIPLINE

Police officers must obey both the law of the land, and their own code of discipline. This discipline code is broken if an officer:

- unreasonably neglects their duty;
- makes a false written or spoken statement;
- misuses their authority, eg through unnecessary violence;
- is rude or abusive;
- is racially discriminatory.

The Police have a legal duty to promote racial equality and good relations between people of different racial groups.

stop & search

Stop!

If a police officer stops you in the street, you are entitled to know the officer's name and the police station where they work. You are also entitled to know why the officer has stopped you. It is not acceptable for this to be simply because of your colour, dress, hairstyle or the fact that you might have been in trouble before.

Strictly speaking, you don't have to answer a police officer's questions, but someone who refuses to give their name and address may well find themselves detained or arrested if the officer believes that they have something to hide.

However, if the police suspect that you have committed an offence then you must give your name, address, date of birth, place of birth and nationality, but need not say any more. The police

officer is entitled to use reasonable force to ensure you remain with him or her while the information you are required to give is checked. You have the right not to answer any more questions until you have received legal advice, see page 111. A police officer can also require any other person they find at a place where they believe an offence has been committed to give the information listed above if the police officer believes they have information relating to that offence.

Stay calm

If you're stopped by the police, keep calm and don't overreact. If you're obstructive and rude, you're more likely to be arrested. Staying calm will also help you remember what happened and what was said. If you deliberately mislead the police by giving false information or wasting their time, you risk a fine or even imprisonment.

Search!

People

The police do not have the power to search anyone they choose, but they can search someone (and the vehicle in which they are travelling), who has been arrested or is suspected of carrying:

- **illegal drugs,;**
- **stolen goods or goods on which duty has not been paid;**
- **offensive weapons, or anything that might be used as a weapon; or**
- **fireworks unlawfully; or**
- **anything that might be used for the hunting or poaching of animals.**

Any search involving more than a check of your outer clothing should be done out of public view or in a police station or van. If the search requires more than the removal of outer clothing, it should be done by someone of the same sex. The way the search is carried out can depend on what the police are looking for. In Scotland, the police do not carry out intimate searches on a person's body.

In the know

If you, or the vehicle in which you are travelling, are searched by the police, the officer should state beforehand why the search is taking place and what they expect to find. You have every right to ask for an explanation if this has not been made clear.

If the police search you illegally, they are committing an assault. But if they have good reason, and you refuse, you may be charged with obstruction.

The police should normally make a written record of the search and tell you how you can obtain a copy.

Special powers

Police powers of search in certain circumstances were extended by the *Criminal Justice and Public Order Act 1994*. If a senior police officer believes that a serious violent incident might take place in the area or that dangerous weapons are being carried, they can give officers the authority to stop any person or vehicle to search for the weapons. This applies even when the constable has no grounds for suspecting that the person stopped might have broken the law.

Property The police do not have the power to enter and search any house or building that they choose. But they are allowed to carry out a search if:

- **they have the agreement of the occupier of the building; or**
- **they have a warrant (or permission) from a court; or**
- **it is necessary due to urgency, e.g., in order to catch an escaped prisoner, save life, prevent serious property damage or to prevent certain kinds of disturbance.**

If possible, the police should explain why they are making the search and should keep a record of whether they needed to use force to get in, any damage caused, and anything they took away.

legal custody

Under the *Criminal Procedure (Scotland) Act 1995* there are two types of situation, namely detention and arrest where the police can take a person under the care and control of the law. This means that for the time being, the suspect loses certain freedoms – such as to go and do as they please – but, in return, has certain rights designed to protect them from unreasonable treatment.

Detention A person may be taken into legal custody so that the police can carry out further investigations, if they do not have enough evidence to bring a charge. If you are detained the police must have reasonable grounds for suspecting you have committed or were committing an offence which is punishable by imprisonment. The police must take you as quickly as possible to a police station or some other premises. The police may only detain you for a maximum time of 6 hours, by the end of which time they must arrest you, detain you on other grounds or release you.

Arrest Arrest is a more serious form of legal custody than detention and a charge should follow on from arrest without undue delay. If you are arrested and taken to a police station, you are entitled to:

- **know the reason for your arrest;**
- **have a solicitor informed;**
- **have someone told where you are.**

You should be told about these rights and cautioned – see page 111.

HELPING THE POLICE WITH THEIR ENQUIRIES

If you are asked to go to a police station to help with enquiries, it's important to know if you are being arrested, or whether the decision to attend is up to you. If you are being asked to go voluntarily, you may refuse – although the police may then decide to detain or arrest you – and then you have to go.

You are entitled to send a message to your family or a friend telling them where you are, and to receive free legal advice from a solicitor, even though you are attending the police station voluntarily.

If you have not been arrested and go to the police station voluntarily, you may leave at any time you wish.

use the law with care try talking first

Legal advice

In almost all circumstances, anyone who has been arrested, or who goes to a police station voluntarily, is entitled to legal advice from the solicitor on duty or one of their own choice. The consultation with the duty solicitor is free and in private.

If you have been arrested or are being questioned about a serious offence, or if you feel at all unsure about your legal position, it is better not to answer questions (except your name, address, date of birth, place of birth and nationality) until you have had a chance to speak to a solicitor.

Questioning

If you are under 16, the police should not normally interview you without your parent or an "appropriate adult" present. An appropriate adult is someone who knows you, such as an adult friend or teacher.

If you have been arrested, you must give the police your name, date of birth, place of birth, address and nationality, but you have the right after that to stay silent and not answer any further questions. However, the court will be told of this if the case goes to trial, and it may strengthen the case against you. If you refuse to answer questions in court, the sheriff, judge or jury are allowed to take this into account in deciding whether you are guilty.

There are clear rules governing the way police officers can question a person, which are designed to stop unfair pressure being placed on a suspect.

There should be regular breaks for food and the cell and interview room should be clean, properly heated, ventilated, and lit. Someone who is deaf or has difficulty in understanding English should be given a signer or an interpreter.

If, after questioning, the police decide to arrest you, they should give you written information about your legal rights.

The caution

Once a police officer has reason to believe that you have committed an offence and wants to question you further they must first caution you by saying: "You are going to be asked questions about (description of crime). You are not bound to answer but, if you do your answers will be noted and may be used in evidence"

at the police station

Tape recording Your interview at the police station may be recorded on tape. The officer will begin with questions about your name and address.

If the interview is not recorded, notes should be made by the officer concerned. You should normally have the opportunity to see these notes and to sign them if you agree that they are a fair record of what was said.

Fingerprints and photographs

The police can take fingerprints and DNA samples (such as hair cuttings or mouth swabs) of anyone who gives their consent or in certain circumstances without their consent. If the person doesn't co-operate, reasonable force can be used. The police are generally allowed to photograph people charged with an offence but must not use force. Fingerprints, DNA samples and photographs must be destroyed if the person is charged and found not guilty, or not charged at all. However, photographs will not be destroyed if the person has a previous conviction.

charge, caution, release

After questioning you, the police must decide what to do next. If there appears to be enough evidence, they can:

- **release you and report the circumstances to the Procurator Fiscal or Children's Reporter who will decide on what action will be taken;**
- **release you on a written signed undertaking (also known as police bail) requiring you to appear at a named court on a named date; or**
- **keep you in custody to appear in court from custody which must be the next day ie not including weekends or court holidays.**

Charged If you are to be charged the wording used by the officer will indicate the nature of the offence and you will also become aware of which of the above methods will be used to progress your case.

Once you are charged you should not be asked any further questions except in certain specified situations, for example, when new information has come to light. If you appear in court from custody, the court must consider the issue of bail on your first appearance. The law states that you should normally be released on bail unless there is good reason to refuse it, for example:

- **because they doubt the truth of the name and address that you have given;**
- **for the protection of others, to stop you committing another offence, or to stop you interfering in their investigations;**
- **for your own protection (or, if you are under 18, because it is in your own interests); or**
- **to make sure you turn up in court.**

Bail If you are granted bail there are standard conditions which must be followed, namely, that you appear at a named court, on a named date and time, that you do not commit an offence while on bail, that you do not interfere with witnesses or otherwise obstruct the course of justice, and that you make yourself available for reports to assist the court in dealing with the offence. The court may also attach special conditions, for example you may be required to report to the police station once a week. If the court refuses or applies conditions to bail it must give the reasons for this decision.

A person who is charged with, or already convicted of, murder, attempted murder, culpable homicide, rape or attempted rape, will only be given bail if the court deciding the matter considers that there are exceptional circumstances that justify doing so. Courts also need not grant bail if it appears that the defendant was already on bail when the offence was committed.

A warning This is a strong warning from the procurator fiscal stating that the nature of the conduct is unacceptable and that the matter could have been sent to court.

Anti-social Behaviour Orders An ASBO, or Anti-social Behaviour Order, is an order issued by a court prohibiting a person from committing specific anti-social acts or from entering a certain area. ASBOs are designed to stop behaviour that causes people distress or alarm, and can be used with anyone aged 12 or above.

The local council will normally apply to a court for an ASBO – and the orders are used to try to control all kinds of anti-social behaviour. An ASBO is effective for a minimum of two years and if it is broken it becomes a criminal offence.

charge, caution, release

Acceptable Behaviour Contracts

An Acceptable Behaviour Contract is an agreement made between a young person, their parent or carer and a local agency, such as the police, social services or a housing authority. The contract will list the kinds of anti-social behaviour that the person promises not to do again, along with any other measures that they (and their parent or carer) agree to undertake.

Fixed Penalty Notices

Police Officers and certain authorised officers have the power to issue a fine, known as a fixed penalty notice, to anyone committing certain offences, for example dropping litter or smoking in no-smoking premises. The fine must be paid within a set period of time specified on the notice and once the fine is paid, the person is no longer liable for conviction and does not receive a criminal record.

COMPLAINTS AGAINST THE POLICE

If you feel that you have suffered, or witnessed police misconduct, you may decide that you want to make an official complaint.

Think about what happened; make sure you are clear what was wrong. If it is a serious matter, it's a good idea to speak to a solicitor or contact your local Citizens' Advice Bureau or MSP or local councillor beforehand. A 'complaints against the police' leaflet should be available at your local police office and will provide information on how the complaint should be made and will be investigated.

You can make your complaint by telephone or letter or in person at a police station.

In reply you may get an apology, or an explanation of the officer's conduct. If you are still not satisfied with how the force has dealt with the complaint you can register your dissatisfaction with Her Majesty's Inspectorate of Constabulary or the Police Complaints Commissioner for Scotland (see Contacts).

use the law with care **try talking first**

Most terrorist offences are already against the law, but the police now have extra powers to help them with their enquiries.

Definition Terrorism refers to actions designed to advance a political, religious or ideological cause, which deliberately…

- **cause serious violence or damage,**
- **threaten or intimidate members of the public,**
- **create a public health or safety risk, or**
- **interfere with electronic communications.**

Police powers The police can use stop and search powers to see if someone is a terrorist even if they do not have any grounds for suspecting the person of committing an offence.

They can specify areas where, for up to 28 days, people and vehicles may be randomly stopped and searched without evidence of illegal activity.

Premises can often be searched without a warrant and a senior police officer can authorise emergency searches if it is believed to be "in the interests of the state".

Areas can be cordoned off to allow the police to search for evidence of terrorism.

Detention Terrorist suspects can be detained by the police without charge for up to 14 days (and this may be extended to 28 days). Access to a solicitor can be delayed for 48 hours.

Under the *Protection of Terrorism Act 2005*, the government can place people

they suspect of terrorism under house arrest, even though they don't have enough evidence to go to court to prove an offence.

Other powers Some organisations are forbidden – known as "proscribed" – which means that it is illegal to be a member of them. The list contains suspected terrorist organisations from around the world.

Since the bomb attacks in London in July 2005, the police have been given extra powers under the *Terrorism Act 2006*. It is now an offence to prepare a terrorist act, to give or receive terrorist training, and to sell or distribute terrorist publications.

"Praising or celebrating" terrorism in a way which could encourage others to carry out a terrorist act can lead to a being arrested and charged with the "glorification of terrorism".

courts

Procurator fiscal and the Crown Office

The job of investigating a crime and charging a suspect is done by the police, but the decision as to whether to continue with the case and bring it to court is made by the procurator fiscal, or the Crown Office when dealing with very serious offences. This is an independent prosecuting service, made up of trained lawyers, who decide whether there is a realistic chance of conviction and whether the seriousness of the crime merits a trial. If the answer to either of these questions is "no", the case will be dropped.

It is difficult to predict the amount of time it will take to investigate and bring a case to court.

Charge or complaint

You will be told of the date and time of your first appearance in court on the written undertaking given to you by the police or on the complaint which will be served on you through the post or by a police officer.

Children's panel and youth court

If you are under 16, or 16–18 and are subject to a supervision order, then your case may be referred to a children's panel hearing. There is also a youth court pilot scheme operating. However, if any child over 8 is charged with an offence, the case may be heard in the district court, the sheriff court or, in serious cases such as murder, in the High Court of Justiciary.

District court

The district court hears criminal cases of a less serious nature (known as summary cases). Normally the case will be heard by a justice of the peace who is usually not legally qualified but a member of the local community. The case may be heard by a stipendiary magistrate who is legally qualified and has higher sentencing powers than a justice of the peace. At present, stipendiary magistrates only sit at Glasgow District Court.

Sheriff court

The sheriff court deals with all criminal cases except murder, rape and treason. The case will be heard by a sheriff.

The sheriff sits alone in less serious cases (known as summary offences) and sits with a jury in more serious cases (known as solemn offences).

There are procedures set out to ensure that a young person accused of a crime is not made to feel intimidated by the experience and receives a fair trial.

High Court of Justiciary

The High Court of Justiciary is the only court that can deal with murder, rape or treason. It can also deal with all serious offences.

The judge, when sitting with a jury, ensures that all matters of law are dealt with correctly but it is for the jury to decide on the facts and reach a verdict.

The sheriff or judge will pass sentence if the defendant is found guilty, and is generally able to impose higher sentences than a district court. The High Court of Justiciary can generally impose higher sentences than the sheriff court. The sentence is decided by taking into account any maximum set by law, the circumstances surrounding the case, previous convictions, and possibly the background of the defendant if it is thought to have any bearing on the case.

Age of criminal responsibility

A child under the age of eight who breaks the law cannot be charged with the crime. However, children under ten who are out of control can be made subject to a child safety order (placing them under the supervision of a social worker or a member of a youth offending team) or a care order (taking them into care).

courts

Legal Aid

Help with the cost of legal advice and the presentation of your case in court is provided by Legal Aid.

If you are charged with an offence, it is important to get legal advice as soon as possible. You may wish to use the solicitor that you saw at the police station, or you can consult another one. Solicitors must hold a contract from the Legal Aid Board in order to carry out this work. You can find a contracted firm by phoning the Legal Aid Board or searching the Legal Aid website, see **contacts**.

There are different types of help available which your solicitor will be able to explain. If you are to be tried in a district court, sheriff court, or the High Court of Justiciary, you may be able to get help with the cost of a solicitor, and possibly an advocate preparing and presenting your case. Depending on your income and savings, you may be required to make a contribution towards the cost.

If you find yourself in court without anyone to give you advice, you can ask to see the duty solicitor who can give you free advice and representation on your first appearance. You could also ask the judge to delay your case until you've had time to talk to someone, though they will probably want to know why you did not sort it out earlier. It is always best if possible to get advice before you go to court.

The Court Service

If you need to go to court, for example as a witness or juror, and need information on what you can expect, or what you might have to do, your local court should be able to help. (See Courts in the phone book), or contact the Scottish Court Service, see **contacts**.

Juries

The job of a jury, which sits in the sheriff court or the High Court of Justiciary is to decide on the facts of a criminal case and on the guilt or innocence of the accused. It is made up of 15 adults (not 12, as in England and Wales), aged between 18–70, who have lived in Britain for a continuous period of at least five years from the age of 13. They are chosen at random from the local electoral register (see page 126), but there are certain categories of people who cannot be selected. These include judges, magistrates, ministers of religion, prison, police and probation officers, anyone on bail or who has been on probation within the last five years, anyone sentenced to prison, detention centre, youth custody or community service within the last ten years.

If you are called as a member of a jury, you will usually be given about six weeks' notice. Although some people, such as MPs, members of the armed forces and the medical profession have the right to be excused, normally it is compulsory. But if there is a strong reason why you are unable to serve – such as exams, a holiday which has been already booked, the care of a relative or major problems at work – then you may be excused or allowed to defer your service until later in the year, although it is important to make this clear as soon as possible.

Jurors are able to claim the cost of travel to court and a small financial allowance. There is information for jurors on the Scottish Court Service websites, see **contacts**.

CONTACTS see pages 142–149 for organisations able to give help & advice

law, government
& human rights

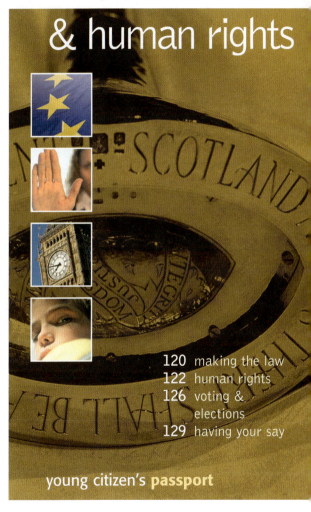

120 making the law
122 human rights
126 voting & elections
129 having your say

young citizen's **passport**

INDIVIDUALS
ENGAGING IN
SOCIETY

Citizenship Foundation

making the law

The Scottish Parliament

The Scottish Parliament began sitting in 1999. It was set up, following a Scotland-wide referendum, by the *Scotland Act 1998*. It is made up of Members of the Scottish Parliament (MSPs). A First Minister is elected by the MSPs and he or she, together with a team of Ministers, forms the Scottish Executive. The Scottish Parliament is able to make laws for Scotland on any subject, except for certain topics which are reserved to the United Kingdom Parliament. The Scottish Parliament also has the power to vary to some extent the rate of income tax which applies to Scottish taxpayers.

A law made by the Scottish Parliament begins its life as a Bill. Bills are put forward by the Scottish Executive, by individual MSPs, or by one of the Scottish Parliament's committees. If the Scottish Parliament votes in favour of the Bill, it will be given the Royal Assent, and is known as an Act of the Scottish Parliament or *asp*. Since its establishment in 1999, the Scottish Parliament has, for example, abolished many forms of hunting with dogs; allowed civil marriage ceremonies to be held outwith Registry Offices; banned smoking inside many premises; and allowed for the creation of National Parks in Scotland. An Act of the Scottish Parliament can, however, be challenged in the Scottish courts if it deals with an area which is reserved to the UK Parliament.

The United Kingdom Parliament

The United Kingdom Parliament sits in Westminster, in London. Only the UK Parliament can pass laws on certain matters, such as the economy, foreign policy, social security, energy, employment, broadcasting, and some medical issues (these are the reserved matters upon which the Scottish Parliament cannot act). In theory, it could still pass laws relating to other Scottish issues, but in practice it would only do so if the Scottish Parliament agrees. All laws for England are still made in the UK Parliament.

The United Kingdom Parliament is made up of two bodies: the House of Commons and the House of Lords. The House of Commons comprises elected Members of Parliament (MPs). The House of Lords is made up of un-elected peers. Bills can be proposed either by the Government (which is led by the Prime Minister) or by an individual MP or peer. The latter are known as *private members' Bills*. To become law, a Bill must be passed by the House of Commons and the House of Lords, and receive the Royal Assent. It is then known as an Act of Parliament. As a general rule, the House of Lords can only delay, but not prevent, a Bill becoming an Act of Parliament. Nor can the Queen refuse to give the Royal Assent.

The Scottish legal system

Scotland has a separate, and different, legal system from England and Wales. In cases in Scotland, the judges will apply Scots law. Scots law is made up of laws passed by the Scottish Parliament, the United Kingdom Parliament, and the old Scottish Parliament (which existed before Scotland united with England in 1707), as well as certain law texts written by Scottish lawyers in the 17th and 18th centuries, and the decisions of other judges in previous cases. Judges do not make new laws, but their decisions may develop the law. Also a specially convened court with a large number of judges can over-rule old cases. Recently a special court of seven judges changed the way that rape is defined in Scotland.

European law

Since the United Kingdom joined the European Community (now the European Union) in 1973, European law has become increasingly important in Scotland. European law is made by the European Parliament, the European Commission, and the Council of Ministers. It covers a wide variety of areas, such as agriculture and employment rights. Sometimes the UK Parliament or the Scottish Parliament will have to pass laws to bring a European law into force in Scotland. Certain types of European legislation are effective, and can be relied upon in Scottish courts, without the Scottish or UK governments having to take any action at all. It is unlawful for the Scottish Parliament to pass any Act of the Scottish Parliament which would be incompatible with European law, and if it did, the Act could be challenged in a Scottish court. Similarly, the Scottish Executive cannot act in breach of European law.

■ BRIEF CASE

brief case

One day in August 1928, Mrs Donoghue went with a friend to a café in Paisley. Her friend bought Mrs Donoghue ginger beer, which came in a dark glass bottle. Mrs Donoghue drank some of the ginger beer. It was only when pouring more of the drink into her tumbler, that she saw that a snail had been in the bottle. Mrs Donoghue sued the manufacturer of the ginger beer in court. She had no contract with the manufacturer, and it was argued that she had no right in law to damages from him. But the House of Lords held that the manufacturer did have a legal duty to the ultimate consumer of his product, in this case, Mrs Donoghue. This case has become the foundation of our law of negligence. The law of negligence allows us in certain circumstances to claim money from people who carelessly cause injury or damage.

human rights

European Convention on Human Rights

The UK is one of the signatories to the European Convention on Human Rights. This Convention was agreed upon by a body called the Council of Europe (to which the UK belongs) and has been in force since 1953. The Convention attempts to protect certain fundamental human rights, for example, the right to life, and the right to a fair trial. A person can take the UK to the European Court of Human Rights in Strasbourg if he or she believes the UK has breached one of the rights protected by the Convention. However, it is now also possible to rely on the Convention in the Scottish courts.

The Scotland Act 1998

Under the *Scotland Act*, the Scottish Parliament cannot pass an Act of the Scottish Parliament which is incompatible with the European Convention on Human Rights. Nor can the Scottish Executive (which includes the Lord Advocate, who is head of the criminal prosecution system in Scotland) take action which would be incompatible with the Convention. Any such Act of the Scottish Parliament or action by the Executive, can be challenged in the Scottish courts, and could be struck down. Since the *Scotland Act* came into force, there have been a number of such challenges. For example, it is now clear that a person cannot be prosecuted by the Lord Advocate for a criminal offence if there has been excessive delay in the criminal proceedings.

■ BRIEF CASE

In September 1976 Jeffrey, aged 16, took a short cut home from his school in Scotland through a nearby cemetery. This was against school rules and Jeffrey was reported to the head, who decided that he should be punished with the strap. The boy refused. He was supported by his parents; who said that they thought corporal punishment was morally wrong. Jeffrey was suspended.

Both the school and the local authority suggested various ways in which he might be allowed back – but could not promise that Jeffrey would never be beaten for misbehaviour. Jeffrey's parents would not agree to this. They claimed that the local authority were breaking part of the European Convention on Human Rights, which says that no one shall be denied the right to education and that parents have the right to make sure that their children are taught in a way that respects their religious and philosophical beliefs.

When the case eventually reached the European Court of Human Rights in 1982, the Court agreed with Jeffrey's mother, who had made the application. As a result, the British government had to change the law on corporal punishment in schools. Corporal punishment was eventually abolished in most UK schools in 1987, and has now been banned in all UK schools.

use the law with care **try talking first**

Human Rights Act 1998

The *Human Rights Act* was brought into force in October 2000. It incorporates most of the human rights set out in the European Convention on Human Rights into the law of Scotland, and of the rest of the UK. Acts of the UK Parliament now have to be read in a way which is compatible with the rights set out in the European Convention on Human Rights. Unlike Acts of the Scottish Parliament, an Act of the UK Parliament cannot be struck down if it is incompatible with the Convention. However, certain courts can declare that the Act is incompatible, and the UK Parliament can then resolve this by altering that law.

The *Human Rights Act* also makes it illegal for a public authority to act incompatibly with the European Convention on Human Rights. Government departments, courts, and local councils are all public authorities. If you believe a public authority has breached your Convention rights you can challenge this by bringing a court action against that public authority. You can also rely on a Convention right in your defence, if a public authority has brought an action against you. You cannot, however, bring a court action against another ordinary citizen alleging that he or she has breached a right protected by the Convention. The courts can order a number of steps, including the payment of a sum of money as damages, if a Convention right has been breached.

The Convention Rights in UK law

There are 16 basic rights in the *Human Rights Act*. They don't only affect matters of life and death like freedom from torture and killing; they also affect people's rights in everyday life: what they can say and do, their beliefs, their right to a fair trial and many other similar basic entitlements.

(Article 1 is introductory)

Article 2 Right to life

Everyone has the absolute right to have their life protected by law. There are only certain very limited circumstances where it is acceptable for the state to take away someone's life, e.g. if a police officer acts justifiably in self-defence.

Article 3 Prohibition of torture

Everyone has the absolute right not to be tortured or subjected to treatment or punishment that is inhuman or degrading.

Article 4 Prohibition of slavery and forced labour

Everyone has the absolute right not to be treated as a slave or forced to perform certain kinds of labour.

Article 5 Right to liberty and security

Everyone has the right not to be deprived of their liberty – "arrested or detained" – except in limited cases specified in the Article (e.g. where they are suspected of or convicted of committing a crime) and where this is justified by a clear legal procedure.

Article 6 Right to a fair trial

Everyone has the right to a fair and public hearing within a reasonable period of time. This applies to both criminal charges and in sorting out cases concerning civil rights and obligations. Hearings must be by an independent and impartial tribunal established by law. It is possible to exclude the public from the hearing (though not the judgment) in order to protect national security or public order. Anyone who is charged with a criminal offence is presumed innocent until proved guilty according to law and has certain guaranteed rights to defend themselves.

Article 7 No punishment without law

Everyone normally has the right not to be found guilty of an offence arising out of actions which at the time they were committed were not criminal. There is also protection against later increases in the possible sentence for an offence.

Articles 8–11

The rights to the following freedoms (in Articles 8–11) may be restricted where this is necessary to protect things like public health or safety, the rights of others or to prevent crime (including racial offences).

Interference with these rights that goes too far can be challenged in the courts who will try to strike a fair balance.

Article 8 Right to respect for private life

Everyone has the right to respect for their private and family life, their home and their correspondence.

Article 9 Freedom of thought, conscience and religion

Everyone is free to hold whatever views, beliefs and thoughts (including religious faith) they like.

Article 10 Freedom of expression

Everyone has the right to express their views on their own or in a group. This applies even if they are unpopular or disturbing. This right can be restricted in specified circumstances.

Article 11 Freedom of assembly and association

Everyone has the right to get together with other people in a peaceful way. They also have the right to associate with other people, which can include the right to form a trade union. These rights may be restricted only in specified circumstances.

Article 12 Right to marry

Men and women have the right to marry and start a family. Our national law still governs how and at what age this can take place.

(Article 13, which deals with legal remedies, is not incorporated into our law)

Article 14 Prohibition of discrimination

Everyone has the right to benefit from these Convention rights regardless of race, religion, sex, political views or any other status, unless a restriction can be reasonably justified.

HOW DOES THE HUMAN RIGHTS ACT AFFECT US?

The *Human Rights Act* is a unique type of higher law, affecting all other laws. The rights and their limitations are a set of basic values. Respect for these rights and everything that goes with them may help change the way people think and behave. It should help create a society in which decisions and policies are better discussed and understood. But the freedoms protected by the Act are not a complete set of human values and do not, for example, include the right to work or freedom from poverty.

The Act cannot be used directly by one private individual against another. It is designed to indicate how judges in courts must interpret the law and how public bodies – such as the police, the prison service and local councils – must carry out their actions.

It protects fundamental freedoms – like liberty and free speech – but at the same time, allows limits to be placed on these rights in order to try to make sure that other people are also treated fairly.

For example, a person's right to liberty may be restricted if they are guilty of a serious crime. This is for other people's protection. Similarly there are limits placed on freedom of speech to prevent someone from shouting 'Fire!' in a crowded hall, when there isn't one.

Article 1 of Protocol 1*
Protection of property

Everyone has the right to the peaceful enjoyment of their possessions. Public authorities cannot usually interfere with things we own or the way we use them, except in specified limited circumstances.

Article 2 of Protocol 1*
Right to education

Everyone has the right not to be denied access to the educational system.

Article 3 of Protocol 1*
Right to free elections

Elections must be free and fair, and take place by secret ballot. Some restrictions can be placed on those who are allowed to vote (e.g. a minimum age).

Articles 1 and 2 of Protocol 6*
Abolition of the death penalty

These provisions abolish the death penalty. There can be limited exceptions in times of war, but only in accordance with clearly specified laws.

* a 'protocol' is a later addition

voting & elections

Who can vote?

Generally if you are 18 or over, and registered to vote, you can vote in the various different types of elections held in Scotland. You must be a citizen of the UK, Republic of Ireland or the Commonwealth to vote in a general election. To be entitled to vote in a local council election, you must live in the local area, and be a citizen of the European Union, the Republic of Ireland, or the Commonwealth. If you are entitled to vote in the Scottish local elections, you can also vote in elections for the Scottish Parliament. Provided that they are living in the UK, nationals of other European countries can vote in elections to the European Parliament. Unlike in some other countries, voting is not compulsory in Scotland. However, it is a very important right.

Who can't vote?

There are certain people who cannot vote in elections in Scotland, for example, people detained in mental institutions, people who do not live in Scotland, and members of the House of Lords.

Registering to vote

Electoral registration forms are sent out to all households in Scotland, gathering information as to which of the persons living there are eligible to vote. This allows the compilation of an electoral register. You must register to vote, if you are entitled to do so, although you need not vote at an election if you do not wish to. Before an election, all registered voters are sent a polling card. This will tell you where you must go to vote (this is known as the polling station, and may often be a local school or similar), and the hours between which the polling station is open. Anyone may choose instead to vote by post. There are also provisions to help people who might have difficulty in casting their vote, for example those with impaired vision.

Methods are being considered to make the process of voting more up-to-date, including mobile polling stations and "e-voting" through the Internet, mobile phones and digital TV.

You can check if your name is on the register of electors at your local main library or council offices.

Who can you vote for?

The candidates standing at an election will usually represent a political party. However, it is also possible for a candidate to stand as an 'independent', not linked to any of the political parties. Currently the Labour Party, the Scottish National Party, the Liberal Democrats, and the Conservative Party all have MPs representing Scottish constituencies at the UK Parliament. A constituency is the area of Scotland which an MP or MSP represents. The Scottish Parliament includes MSPs representing the Labour Party, the Scottish National Party, the Scottish Conservative & Unionist Party, the Scottish Liberal Democrats, the Scottish Green Party, the Scottish Socialist Party, Solidarity and the Scottish Senior Citizens Unity Party, as well as a number of 'independent' MSPs. Sometimes a candidate might campaign largely on one particular issue. For example, the Scottish Parliament currently includes a representative of the Scottish Senior Citizens Unity Party, and a doctor who campaigned to save a local hospital from closure.

Local elections

There used to be two tiers of local councils in Scotland, but this is no longer the case, and there is now just one local council for every area. These local authorities provide services such as education, social work, and refuse collection, in their local area. Councillors are elected to represent a particular community, known as a ward, on the local council. Local elections are now to be held every four years, at the same time as the Scottish Parliament elections. In the past, a 'first past the post' method of voting has been used. However, for the council elections in 2007 and thereafter, a number of councillors are to be elected for each ward, using a form of 'proportional representation'.

LOCAL COUNCILLOR, MSP, MP OR MEP?

If you are over 21, you are generally able to stand for election. However, it is planned that this minimum age should be lowered to 18 for election as an MP, and the minimum age has already been lowered to 18 for standing as a councillor. To seek election as a councillor, you must also have a link with the local authority area, for example, you are a voter, or stay or work, there. If you reside in Scotland but are a citizen of another EU state you can stand for election as an MSP, although you cannot seek election as an MP. You will need to put forward a deposit if you wish to stand for election as an MSP, MP or MEP. For would-be MSPs and MPs, the deposit is currently £500, and this is forfeited if you receive under 5% of all the votes cast. A deposit of £5,000 is required for MEPs. Usually most candidates represent political parties, which have their own selection procedures to choose candidates for election.

voting & elections

Scottish Parliament elections

MSPs are elected to the Scottish Parliament every four years. The voting system for these elections is a form of 'proportional representation'. Scotland is split into both constituencies and regions (a region is a group of constituencies). When voting, you are given two ballot papers. On the first you choose who you would like to be the MSP for your constituency. The second ballot paper is the regional one, and you are simply asked to vote for a political party (or independent candidate). Depending on the results of both ballots, the political parties are allocated a certain number of extra MSPs in each region. This system is designed to ensure that the number of MSPs any political party has in the Parliament, reflects the proportion of Scottish people who voted for that party. There are currently 73 constituency MSPs, and 56 regional list MSPs, in the Scottish Parliament.

This system of voting has allowed the election of representatives from smaller parties, such as the Scottish Green Party. It has also resulted in no one political party having an overall majority in the Scottish Parliament. The largest party in the Parliament is not able to win a parliamentary vote if all the other parties join together in opposition. Two of the political parties have therefore agreed to work together and form a coalition.

MSPs debate and pass legislation on certain Scottish issues. They also work on parliamentary committees. They can ask questions on your behalf in the Scottish Parliament, or contact the appropriate Minister in the Scottish Executive about an issue that you have raised.

General elections

The election of MPs to the UK Parliament is commonly called a general election. The date on which it is held is decided by the Prime Minister who can call a general election at any time, and there must be one at least every five years. MPs are still selected using a 'first past the post' system, although there has been debate about whether this should be replaced in the future with a system of proportional representation. Presently, there are 646 MPs sitting at Westminster, of which 59 represent Scottish constituencies. The political party with the largest number of MPs after an election becomes the Government. The leader of that party is the Prime Minister. He or she appoints a number of MPs as ministers, who each have different responsibilities, such as the economy, or Scottish affairs at Westminster.

Like MSPs, MPs will debate and vote on possible legislation, work on committees, and can raise issues for you in the UK Parliament.

European elections

Elections to the European Parliament, which sits in both Strasbourg and in Brussels, are held every five years. A system of proportional representation is used to select the MEPs who are to represent Scotland. All the countries that are members of the European Union elect MEPs to sit in the European Parliament. MEPs are involved in making European law, see **the european union**, pages 139–141.

Campaigning

If you feel strongly about something and want to get involved yourself, a library, Citizens' Advice Bureau, or one of the organisations or websites listed in the **contacts** section can probably give you some of the information you need to find out who to contact.

This ranges from individual action to something more co-ordinated, as a member of a group. Letter writing is the usual starting point – do your research, send it to a named person (the most senior within the organisation), keep a copy, and try to get others involved as well. If you can get a letter published in a newspaper, many more will know about your views, but do give your name and address · although you can ask the paper not to publish it.

Freedom of Information

Under the *Freedom of Information (Scotland) Act 2002*, anybody can ask for information from public authorities in Scotland, such as the Scottish Executive, local government, police, and the National Health Service.

Your request must:

- **be in writing (or some other form which could be kept for the future);**
- **state clearly what information is required; and must also include**
- **your full name and address.**

The department or organisation must respond to your request as soon as possible, and in not more than 20 working days. There may be a charge for this service. Your request may be refused for security reasons, or if provision of the information would cost in excess of a prescribed sum.

Reuqests for information from UK central government are governed by the *Freedom of Information Act 2000*, but the rules relating to such requests are very similar to those outlined above for Scottish public authorities.

See **contacts** for futher help and information.

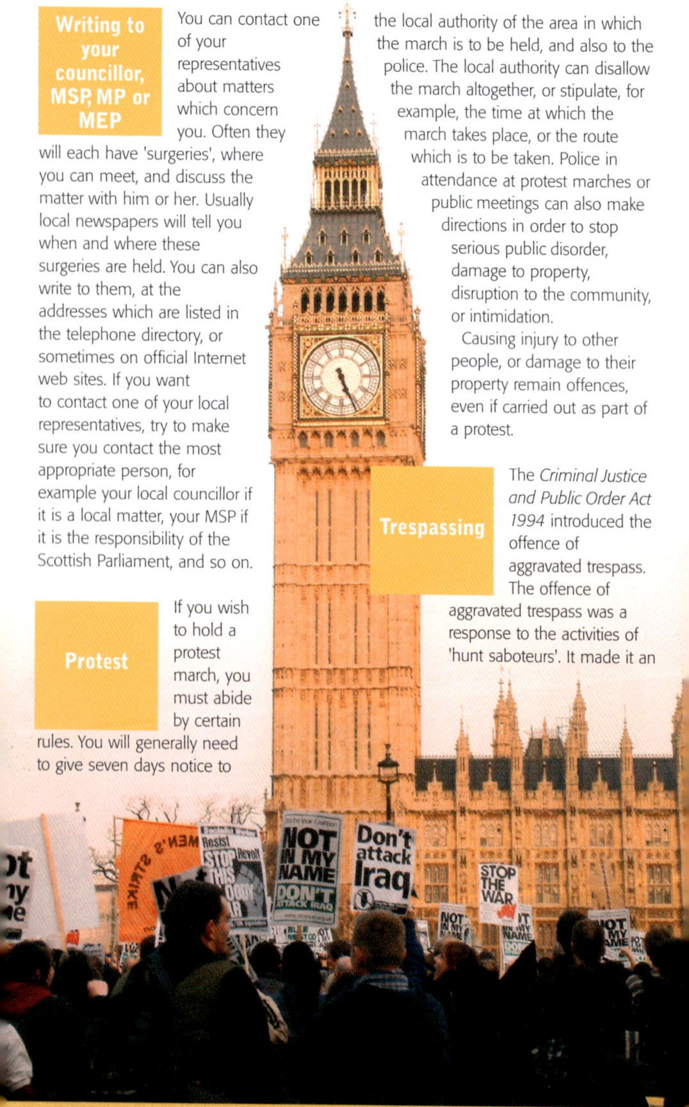

having your say

Writing to your councillor, MSP, MP or MEP

You can contact one of your representatives about matters which concern you. Often they will each have 'surgeries', where you can meet, and discuss the matter with him or her. Usually local newspapers will tell you when and where these surgeries are held. You can also write to them, at the addresses which are listed in the telephone directory, or sometimes on official Internet web sites. If you want to contact one of your local representatives, try to make sure you contact the most appropriate person, for example your local councillor if it is a local matter, your MSP if it is the responsibility of the Scottish Parliament, and so on.

Protest

If you wish to hold a protest march, you must abide by certain rules. You will generally need to give seven days notice to the local authority of the area in which the march is to be held, and also to the police. The local authority can disallow the march altogether, or stipulate, for example, the time at which the march takes place, or the route which is to be taken. Police in attendance at protest marches or public meetings can also make directions in order to stop serious public disorder, damage to property, disruption to the community, or intimidation.

Causing injury to other people, or damage to their property remain offences, even if carried out as part of a protest.

Trespassing

The *Criminal Justice and Public Order Act 1994* introduced the offence of aggravated trespass. The offence of aggravated trespass was a response to the activities of 'hunt saboteurs'. It made it an offence to try to intimidate, obstruct or disrupt the lawful activities of others in certain situations. In fact, however, the Scottish Parliament has now passed legislation banning many types of hunting with dogs, such as fox hunting.

Complaining

If you have a complaint about something you have bought or a service you have received, it's important to act quickly. Some companies, and many public services, have special procedures for dealing with complaints. If it's a public service, such as a hospital or benefits agency, you can ask to see a copy of their charter which shows the level of service you are entitled to expect. If your complaint is not dealt with properly, think about contacting your local councillor, MSP or MP, particularly if your problem is over a public service.

- **act as quickly as possible;**
- **think carefully about what you want to achieve and if necessary get advice;**
- **make sure you talk or write directly to a person – such as the manager or director of services – who has the authority to deal with your complaint;**
- **always find out the name of the person you are talking to;**
- **keep a record of phone calls or letters that you send;**
- **stick to the facts, and work out how the law can help you;**
- **state clearly what you want to be done, set a reasonable time within which this should happen, and get back in touch if they haven't met the deadline.**

If you are still unhappy with the way your problem has been handled, you may be able to take your case to an Ombudsman. See **contacts**, page 142.

Data Protection

How can I check what they know about me?

People collect personal information about you all the time. Your school, your GP, the local council, shops, your mobile phone company, your bank, your employer, the police and many others all keep records on you. Sometimes it's facts like your age or how much you've spent on your mobile phone; sometimes it's opinions about say a health risk or whether you might commit an offence or fail an exam.

The *Data Protection Act 1998* says that this can be done as long as the people keeping and using the information follow various rules and regulations. The law tries to balance your right to privacy and fair treatment with other people's legitimate rights to keep and use information about you.

Very strict rules apply to other people collecting and using personal information such as your racial or ethnic origins, your political, religious, or other views, your sex life, any criminal offences and the state of your health. Usually your clear consent is needed before this information is stored or used.

One of the main protections you have is to be able to check what information is held about you and to get it put right if it's wrong.

You are known as a "data subject" and the law says you can apply to anyone to ask if they hold information about you, and if so what it is, by making a "subject access request".

Applying for information You can write this in your own words, asking for all personal information held about you. Some organisations like the police have their own forms which you should use. You should identify yourself clearly and be as specific as possible about what you want to know. You can be asked to pay a fee. This is normally £10 but in some cases it can be as little as £2 (for credit information) or as much as £50 (for old handwritten medical records and some education records). You should get a reply within 40 days (again in some cases shorter times must be met). If you think the information is wrong you can require that it is changed and if necessary go to court for an order to correct inaccurate information. Full details of your rights to check information held about you are available from The Information Commissioner's website – see **contacts**.

Judicial review It is possible in some circumstances for decisions and acts of government departments and public bodies to be struck down in court, for example, if they are unlawful or irrational. This is done by raising a petition for judicial review in the Court of Session in Edinburgh. The decisions of local councils, tribunals (such as immigration tribunals), and certain other bodies (for example the Scottish Football Association) can all be subjected to judicial review. This is a difficult area of law, and therefore you should seek advice from a solicitor.

the european union

134 membership
135 the single market
136 travel & work
137 goods
138 governing europe
140 law makers

young citizen's **passport**

INDIVIDUALS
ENGAGING IN
SOCIETY

Citizenship Foundation

membership

There are currently 27 countries belonging to the European Union:

Austria, Belgium, Bulgaria, the Czech Republic, Cyprus, Denmark, Estonia, Finland, France, Germany, Greece, Hungary, Ireland, Italy, Latvia, Lithuania, Luxembourg, Malta, the Netherlands, Poland, Portugal, Romania, Slovakia, Slovenia, Spain, Sweden, and the United Kingdom.

It is expected that negotiations will also take place with Croatia, Macedonia and Turkey but it is expected that further enlargement will be slower than in recent years.

Origins After the end of the Second World War, governments throughout Europe were determined not to repeat the horrors of the War, in which 50 million people had died.

Beginnings In 1951, France, Belgium, Italy, Luxembourg, the Netherlands, and West Germany signed an agreement setting up the European Coal and Steel Community through which the coal and steel production of all six countries came under the control of a single European authority.

The architects of this plan believed that placing coal and steel production outside the control of individual states would greatly reduce the likelihood of another war. Britain was invited to join the ECSC, but declined.

Growth In the early years co-operation was mainly designed to make it easier for member states to trade with one another. Gradually, the scope of the union has widened, and covers many areas today, including employment, the environment, transport, travel, foreign policy – and for thirteen of the member states a common currency – the euro.

use the law with care try talking first

The idea of European states forming a single market has always been central to the development of the European Union.

A single market means that goods, services, people, and money must be able to move freely between member states.

Over the last 30 years member states have agreed all kinds of measures to make this possible:

- **taxes and duties on products have been made broadly similar between member states;**
- **technical and safety specifications of goods have been standardised, so that goods made in one state meet the standards required in another;**
- **people are allowed to travel, live, study, and work more-or-less wherever they wish.**

A single currency

The EU has also eased the movement of goods and people through the creation of a single currency, also sometimes called economic and monetary union (EMU).

The idea was first proposed in 1969, but the first significant steps were not taken until around 1990 when member states interested in moving towards a single currency began to prepare their economies for this process.

They were required to meet a number of conditions – usually described as convergence criteria – such as having low interest rates, keeping currency rates and prices stable and keeping government expenditure within certain limits.

The euro

On 1st January 2002, after a transition period of two years, twelve of the 15 EU member states moved to a single currency – the euro (€).

Since 28th February 2002, euro banknotes and coins have been the sole legal tender within these 12 countries. In January 2007. the euro was also adopted in Slovenia.

The seven euro notes, from €5 – €500 are the same throughout the single currency area. Each country produces its own coins, of smaller value, although these can be used anywhere within the euro area, regardless of national origin.

Britain and the euro

Britain, Denmark, and Sweden decided not to proceed with the single currency. Denmark has held two national referendums on joining the euro, rejecting the idea on both occasions. In 2003, the people of Sweden voted against the euro. The British government has also undertaken to hold a referendum on the issue when the government believes that its own five convergence criteria have been met.

travel & work

Measures have been gradually introduced to help people move around the EU as easily as possible.

Travel

Citizens of an EU member state have the right to travel to any EU country, if they have a valid passport or identity card. This right may be restricted only for reasons of public order, public security, or public health.

EU citizens also have the right to travel within the EU with members of their family, but if they do not have EU nationality they may be required to have a visa, in addition to their passport.

Border controls

There are no customs checks for people travelling from one EU member state to another – although police controls on some frontiers remain, checking for terrorist activity, drug-trafficking and organised crime.

In addition, identity checks for EU citizens have been abolished at many borders, under what is called the Schengen Agreement. This allows people to travel from one country to another without having their passport or identity documents examined. All member states except Britain and Ireland have joined this group.

Health care

Citizens of EU member states who fall ill within another EU country are entitled to emergency treatment under that country's health scheme.

The treatment is free to someone from Britain who can show the medical authorities their European Health Insurance Card (see page 96).

A person who does not have an EHIC is still entitled to treament, but may be asked to pay its full cost.

Help

An EU citizen who gets into difficulties in a country outside the EU may seek protection from the embassy or consulate of any EU member state.

For example, a British student arrested in a Russian city without a British consular office is entitled to help from the Swedish or Finnish consulate.

use the law with care try talking first

Work

British citizens are entitled to work in any EU country, and should be offered employment under the same conditions as citizens of that state. It would be against the law, for example, for an Italian firm to require British job applicants to have higher qualifications than their Italian counterparts – and vice versa.

Most jobs are open to all EU citizens. However, member states are allowed to insist that only nationals of that state hold certain public service posts, such as those in the police or armed forces. A residence permit is required for anyone who wants to stay in another member state for more than three months. This requires ID and evidence of financial support.

Conditions

Generally speaking, a British citizen working in an EU member state has exactly the same employment rights and duties as everyone else in that country, and it is against the law for that person to be discriminated against on grounds of their nationality.

A British worker in Berlin, for example, should receive the same pay, employment opportunities, and health and safety protection as his or her German counterparts.

Qualifications

The EU operates on the system that someone qualified to work in a particular profession in their own country is also able to carry out that work in any other member state. However not all qualifications are automatically recognised – although applicants are able to check if their particular diploma or certificate is recognised.

Benefits

Citizens of EU member states are entitled to the same welfare and social security benefits as nationals of the country where they are working. This covers sickness and maternity benefits, benefits for accidents at work and unemployment. They also have the same rights, where it is available, to accommodation, such as local authority housing.

Taxes

A person who lives and works in an EU member state must normally pay taxes in the same way as any other resident of that country. Levels of taxation vary from one EU state to another, but work is under way to try to find ways of harmonising taxation across member states.

goods

Customs duties

Generally speaking, goods purchased by people for their own use may be bought in other member states and brought back to Britain without having to pay extra tax or duties. People can bring in as much tobacco and alcohol from other EU member states as they like, as long as it is for personal use only and not for resale. But there is a limit of 200 cigarettes if travelling from the Czech Republic, Estonia, Hungary, Latvia, Lithuania, Poland, Slovakia and Slovenia. Customs officials in the UK have the right to stop people and check this, and to confiscate any items they believe are not for personal use.

governing europe

The structure of the government of the European Union is not easy to understand – possibly because there are several organisations that help to determine EU policy.

THE EUROPEAN COUNCIL

The European Council is the name given to the regular meetings between the heads of the member states. They decide the issues the European Union should be concerned with. In the past this has included unemployment, drug trafficking, and enlarging the EU.

The Council of Ministers

The Council of Ministers is one of the most influential bodies in the EU. It consists of government ministers from each member state with powers to adopt new laws, take decisions about how the EU is run, recommend policy, and negotiate with non-member states on behalf of the EU. It's at the centre of government in the EU, rather like the Cabinet is in Britain.

Decisions

Until the mid 1980s, decisions by the Council of Ministers tended to have to be unanimous. If a nation disagreed, the measure could not be passed. Today the Council generally uses a system called qualified majority voting. Each member state has a certain number of votes, broadly reflecting the size of the country in terms of its population.

For example, France, Germany, Italy, and the United Kingdom have 29 votes. Smaller countries, like Cyprus and Latvia, have four.

The European Commission

Based in Brussels, the European Commission is rather like the civil service of the European Union, taking care of the day-to-day running of the organisation. Almost 30,000 people work for the Commission, making it one of Europe's largest institutions.

The Commission does several different jobs. It:

- **drafts proposals for new EU laws or policies;**
- **checks that EU laws and treaties are properly applied;**
- **begins legal action against member states or businesses that it believes are not following EU law.**

EU Commissioners

Each member state appoints one or two commissioners to take responsibility for running one particular aspect of EU business.

There are 27 Commissioners in all. The current President, José Manuel Barroso is from Portugal, and former Labour MP, Peter Mandelson, is the UK representative. Currently he is EU Commissioner for Trade.

Proposed EU Constitution

In 2004, leaders of EU Member States, including the British Prime Minister, agreed a draft constitution, which was to be ratified, or approved by, every EU country through either Parliament or a referendum over the next two years.

The constitution sets out the rights of all EU citizens and indicates what the EU can and cannot do. It lays down the way in which decisions will be taken and commits the EU to a common foreign and defence policy.

Sixteen member states have now approved the proposed constitution – but it has been rejected by France and the Netherlands, two EU founder-member countries. Although the 2006 deadline has not been met, further discussions are taking place over how to proceed.

The European Parliament

The European Parliament currently consists of 786 MEPs (Members of the European Parliament). The Parliament meets in Brussels, Luxembourg and Strasbourg.

In the course of a month, MEPs usually meet for one week in Strasbourg, and for two weeks, on committee work, in Brussels. Parliamentary support staff are based in Brussels and Luxembourg.

Powers Today, MEPs:
- **decide, together with the Council of Ministers, on EU law;**
- **control more than half the money that the EU spends;**
- **watch over the European Commission and approve the appointment of all Commissioners.**

Elections The UK is allocated 78 of the 786 seats in the European Parliament. At the last election in 2004, the Conservatives were the largest UK party in the European Parliament.

Voting In the UK, as in all other EU member states, voting in European Parliamentary elections is open to any EU citizen, provided they are on the local register of electors.

Contact Debates in the European Parliament are open to the public, and groups and individuals can visit the Parliamentary building. MEPs may be reached by e-mail or by post or phone at their constituency office.

Petitions All EU citizens have the right to submit a petition to the President of the European Parliament (the address is Rue Wiertz, B-1047, Brussels) or online giving their view on a matter that is within the remit of the EU. The petition can be in any form – as long as it contains the sender's name, address, occupation, and signature.

■ BRIEF CASE

In 1999, the European Parliament ordered an investigation into fraud and corruption by members of the European Commission. The report of the investigation was very critical of the Commission and led to all 20 Commissioners resigning.

■ BRIEF CASE

Following a recent successful petition to the EU, the Greek authorities are now required to admit EU citizens to their museums under the same conditions as Greek nationals.

The law in Scotland is still created and developed by MPs (and now MSPs) and judges.

However, our membership of the European Union requires all our laws to follow the treaties and agreements that we have made as members of the EU.

In this sense European law has become the most important source of law in Britain. This is not to say that all our law comes from Europe, but it does mean that all our current and future laws must not break the principles set out in the treaties that we have signed.

■ BRIEF CASE: Mr Litster

Mr Litster worked for a Scottish company, which became insolvent. At 3.30pm one afternoon, Mr Litster and his colleagues were sacked. At 4.30pm that afternoon, a new company took over the business of the company which had become bankrupt. It offered to take on the employees of the old company, but at lower wages. The UK Government had adopted European laws to protect employees in these types of situations, but courts in the UK had previously said these only applied if the the employee was sacked at exactly the same time as the transfer of business. The House of Lords looked at judgements of the European Court of Justice and decided that this was not correct, and that Mr Litster was entitled to compensation.

The European Union

Law created through our membership of the European Union normally reaches us in four ways – through treaties, regulations, directives, and court judgements.

Treaties

Treaties are agreements made between our government and other EU member states, which become incorporated into our law by Parliament. Treaties often contain broad agreements on which further action will be based. Sometimes, however, they include sections that can have a very specific effect on people's lives.

■ BRIEF CASE

The Treaty of Rome, signed in 1957, is the agreement upon which the European Economic Community was established. Article 119 of the Treaty states that men and women should receive equal pay for equal work.

CONTACTS see pages 142–149 for organisations able to give help & advice

Regulations Regulations are the laws that put treaties into practice.

■ BRIEF CASE

An important section of the Treaty of Rome says that people should be able to move freely for work between member states. The regulations that have followed the Treaty require member states to introduce new laws to ensure this works. As a result, all member states needed to have laws granting visiting EU workers the same rights to education and housing as the citizens of their own state.

Directives Directives, like regulations, are a means of putting an EU objective into practice, but member states are able to choose for themselves how this will be done.

■ BRIEF CASE

In 2001, the EU issued a directive requiring companies operating in the EU to inform employees about any decision affecting their jobs – especially if it might lead to redundancy. This directive was made following a number of unexpected redundancies in France, issued by several multi-national companies. The UK was given seven years in which to implement the directive.

Court judgements The European Court of Justice considers all matters of European Community law. Located in Luxembourg, it is the most senior court in Europe and overrules all national courts. Member states must follow its decisions.

■ BRIEF CASE: John

Until recently, UK winter fuel payments were paid to women from the age 60, but not to men until they reached 65. This was challenged in the English High Court by retired postman John Taylor, who claimed it was unlawful discrimination. The English High Court asked the European Court of Justice to deliver a judgement on this in the light of European Community law. The European Court announced that this practice did not follow community law and that winter fuel payments should be given to men and women under the same terms.

Getting information & advice

- Before you write, phone or ask for information, think carefully about exactly what you need to know.
- Don't be overlong in your explanation, keep to the most important details.
- If you are telephoning, you will probably first speak to a receptionist who may not be able to answer your question. Explain that you'd like to talk to someone about…(name the subject), and you should be put through. If they can't help, they may be able to give you the name of someone who can.
- It sometimes helps to put a few key words down on paper to remind you of what you want to say. You may also need a pen and paper to make a note of what you are told.
- It's a good idea to ask who you are talking to so, if you write or phone again, you know the name of the person you first spoke to.

The following names and details are arranged according to the chapters in the main part of the book and are just a few of the many organisations that can help with the whole range of law-related problems.

General

Childline Scotland, Freepost 1111, 18 Albion Street, Glasgow G1 1LH. A dedicated bullying helpline, tel 0800 441 111, open 3.30pm and 9.30pm on weekdays. **www.childline.org.uk**

Citizens' Advice Bureau, or CAB, gives free, confidential and independent advice and advice on all kinds of problems. You can enquire by phone or at one of their offices in most towns and cities. For your nearest CAB, see the local phone book, **www.nacab.org.uk** and for advice **www.adviceguide.org.uk/scotland**

Law Society of Scotland, 26 Drumsheugh Gardens, Edinburgh EH3 7HR, tel 0131 226 7411 email: lawscot@lawscot.org.uk, provides information on using a solicitor. The Society is also responsible for dealing with complaints made against solicitors **www.lawscot.org.uk**.

Liberty, 21 Tabard Street, London SE1 4LA, tel 020 7403 3888. A campaigning organisation able to answer questions from people who feel their civil liberties have been infringed. An advice line is open on Mondays and Thursdays, 6.30–8.30pm, Wed 12.30–2.30pm, tel 0845 123 2307, **www.liberty-human-rights.org.uk**. Liberty's

other website, **www.yourrights.org.uk**, provides further information on human rights and the law

The Ombudsman. If you have a problem with your local authority, a government department, the health service, an insurance company, a bank or building society or a legal service, and are not happy with how your complaint has been dealt with, you can refer your case to the relevant Ombudsman.

You must first, however, have done everything you can to sort things out yourself with the person or organisation concerned. Your local CAB can explain how to submit a complaint, or you can contact the appropriate office at one of the addresses below. If the Ombudsman decides your complaint is reasonable, the department or organisation responsible will be asked to do something about it – which might mean that you get an apology or compensation. New procedures may also be put into place to make sure the same thing doesn't happen again.

Scottish Public Services Ombudsman, 4 Melville Street, Edinburgh,EH3 7NS, Tel 0870 011 5378 E-mail: enquiries@scottishombudsman.org.uk deals with complaints about Scottish public bodies (ie, health service, local government, housing associations) and investigates complaints relating to mental health and complaints against Scottish Enterprise and Highlands and Island Enterprise **www.scottishombudsman.org.uk**

Parliamentary Ombudsman Millbank Tower, Millbank, London SW1P 4QP, tel 0845 015 4033.

Scottish Legal Services Ombudsman, 17 Waterloo Place, Edinburgh EH1 3DL, tel 0131 556 9123, email: ombudsman@slso.org.uk. If you have complained to the Law Society of Scotland about a solicitor, but you are not happy with the way your complaint was handled you can ask the Legal Services Ombudsman to investigate. **www.slso.org.uk**

Scottish Child Law Centre, 54 East Crosscauseway, Edinburgh EH8 9HD. Offers advice on a wide range of issues by letter, phone and text. The advice line is open Mon–Wed and Fri 9.30am–4pm, Thurs 6–7.30pm, tel 0800 328 8970. Or text 'SCLC' and your question to 80800 for free advice by text.

Scottish Legal Aid Board, 44 Drumsheugh Gardens, Edinburgh EH3 7SW, tel 0131 226 7061, email: general@slab.org.uk. Legal aid allows people who would not otherwise be able to afford it, to get help with their legal problems **www.slab.org.uk**

Solicitors give advice on legal problems, take action for you on your behalf and represent you in many courts or tribunals (they may engage an advocate – the equivalent to a barrister in England and Wales – to appear in higher courts). See **www.advocates.org.uk**

There are solicitors' offices in almost every town and city in Scotland. Many solicitors take publicly funded or conditional fee cases, and some will give you a free introductory interview. However when you first make contact, it's important to check that legal aid is available and if not, ask how much the work will cost. Choosing the right firm of solicitors is important. The Law Society of Scotland or your local CAB can give you the name of firms specialising in cases involving your particular problem.

Young Scot provides a wide range of services to young Scots, in collaboration with the Scottish Executive and all local authorities. Comprehensive free booklets are available which offer guidance and advice in many areas of life, and the Young Scot card offers Scottish – and European – wide discounts on shopping, services and travel. The website offers many further resources. Young Scot, Rosebery House, 9 Haymarket Terrace, Edinburgh EH12 5EZ, tel 0131 313 2488 **www.youngscot.org**

Youth Access, 1–2 Taylor's Yard, 67 Alderbrook Road, London SW12 8AD, tel 020 8772 9900, email: admin@youthaccess.org.uk If you have a problem of any kind you would like to discuss confidentially, Youth Access can put you in touch with someone locally who may be able to help. There is no charge for their service.

YouthLink Scotland, Rosebery House, 9 Haymarket Terrace, Edinburgh EH12 5EZ, tel 0131 313 2488. National youth agency for Scotland, promoting the well-being and development of young people in Scotland in partnership with national and local government, the voluntary sector, and the business community **www.youthlink.co.uk**

Websites on the law. A good set of links to websites on all sorts of law is at **www.scottishlawreports.org.uk/ resources/links/links.html**

Life

HEALTH

MIND, Granta House, 15–19 Broadway London E15 4BQ, tel 020 8519 2122, is a leading mental health charity in England and Wales able to give information and advice on a range of mental health issues. Mindinfoline, tel 0845 766 0163, Mon–Fri 9.15am–5.15pm, **www.mind.org.uk**

NHS 24, a 24hr helpline providing confidential advice to anyone concerned about their health, or with questions about any aspect of the Health Service in Scotland, tel 08454 24 24 24. **www.nhs24.com**

Samaritans, will talk to anyone feeling desperate, lonely or suicidal. You can say what you like, you need not give your name, it's entirely confidential. They can be reached by phone at any time, every day of the year. The central number is 08457 90 90 90 or, for your local branch, look under 'S' in the phone book. **www.samaritans.org.uk**

Sane, 1st Floor, Cityside House, 40 Adler Street, London E1 1EE, tel 020 7375 1002, able to provide information and advice to anyone (including friends and family) suffering mental health problems. They can also give callers the names of solicitors prepared to give up to an hour's free advice and put them in touch with support available in their local area. A helpline operates every day of the year, tel 0845 767 8000, 1–11pm, **www.sane.org.uk**

Scottish Association for Mental Health, Cumbrae House, 15 Carlton Court, Glasgow G5 9JP, tel 0141 568 7000. Information Centre opening hours, 2–4.30pm Monday to Friday, tel 0141 568 7000, email: info@samh.org.uk. Also offer free legal advice. **www.samh.org.uk**

DRUGS AND ADDICTION

Alcohol Concern, First Floor, 8 Shelton Street, London WC2H 9JR, tel, 020 7395 4000, provides information on all aspects of alcohol misuse, including details of local alcohol advice and counselling services, **www.alcoholconcern.org.uk**

Drinkline, a confidential advice and helpline for those with drink related concerns, tel (freephone) 0800 917 82 82.

DrugScope, 32–36 Loman Street, London SE1 0EE, tel 020 7928 1211. Information about drug advice agencies in your area. **www.drugscope.org.uk**

FRANK, a website www.talktofrank.com and a 24hr free confidential helpline providing advice and information on all types of drug taking for drug users, their family and friends, tel 0800 77 66 00. A translator for non-English speakers is available at all times, covering 120 languages, textphone 0800 9178765, email: frank@talktofrank.com

Know The Score, free information line 0800 587 5879. Website provides you with all the facts on drugs in Scotland.
www.knowthescore.info

Narcotics Anonymous, tel 020 7730 0009 or 0845 3733366, a confidential helpline, open 10am–10pm, 7 days a week, for those trying to recover from addiction. **www.ukna.org**

Release, 388 Old Street, London EC1V 9LT, information and legal advice service on drug-related problems. A helpline is open Mon–Fri 11am–1pm, tel 0845 4500 215,
www.release.org.uk

SEX, FAMILY PLANNING, CONTRACEPTION, PREGNANCY AND ABORTION

AFLaGA, BCM Box 8431, London WC1N 3XX, can give advice and support to serving and ex-serving members of the armed forces who are lesbian or gay. The helpline, tel 0870 740 7755, operates Wed 7–9pm & Sun 9am–7pm, but messages can also be left outside this time. **www.aflaga.org.uk**

British Agencies for Adoption and Fostering, Scottish Centre, 40 Shandwick Place, Edinburgh, EH2 4RT, tel 0131 220 4749, email: Scotland@baaf.org.uk offer advice and information on adoption and fostering and can put you in touch with an office near you. **www.baaf.org.uk**

British Pregnancy and Advisory Service, has over 40 centres nationwide able to provide pregnancy tests, consultation and emergency contraception, and to undertake abortions. For BPA's Actionline tel 0845 7 30 40 30. Mon–Fri 8.00am–9.00pm, Saturday 8.30am–6.00pm, Sunday, 9.30am–2.30pm.
www.bpas.org

Brook Advisory Centres, offer free and confidential advice and counselling on sex and contraception for young people under 25, covering the whole of the UK. An advice line is open Mon– Fri 9am–5pm, tel 0800 0185 023. If you are under 19, you can call Sexwise from 7.00am–12 midnight (daily) on 0800 28 29 30. **www.brook.org.uk**; 24 hour recorded info, tel 020 7950 7700.

Caledonia Youth, 5 Castle Terrace, Edinburgh EH1 2DP, tel 0131 229 3596, provides free confidential advice and counselling on sex and contraception for young people under 25, email: edinburgh.information@caledoniayouth.org. **www.caledoniayouth.org**

fpa, Unit 10, Firhill Business Centre, 76 Firhill Road, Glasgow G20 7BA, runs a contraceptive eduation helpline, tel 0141 576 5088 (open Monday to Thursday 9am–5pm, Friday 9am–4.30pm). **www.fpa.org.uk**

LIFE 24 hour helpline, Life is an organisation that campaigns against abortion. It offers help and advice to women who do not wish to have an unwanted pregnancy terminated, tel 01926 311 511. **www.lifeuk.org**

Stonewall Scotland, c/o The LGB Centre, 11 Dixon Street, Glasgow G1 4AZ, tel 0141 204 0746, email: calum.irving@stonewall.org.uk. Campaigns for equality for lesbians, gay men and bisexuals and can provide information on these issues.
www.stonewallscotland.org.uk

HIV AND AIDS

The 1990 Trust, Suite 12 Winchester House, 9 Cranmer Road, London SW9 6EJ, tel 020 7582 1990, provides information for people of African, Asian and Caribbean extraction on a variety of health and many other issues including HIV/AIDS. **www.blink.org.uk**.

Avert, 4 Brighton Road, Horsham, West Sussex, RH13 5BA, tel 01403 210202, an international HIV and AIDS charity based in the UK, providing education and information to communities throughout the world including the UK. The website gives details of local UK community organisations where direct advice and help is available.
www.avert.org/aidsuk.htm

National AIDS Helpline, a 24hr freephone service, staffed by advisors who can deal with questions on sex, drugs or relationships, tel 0800 567 123.

Positively Women, 347–349 City Road, London EC1V 1LR, tel 020 7713 0444, helpline 020 7713 1020, 10am–1pm and 2–4pm Mon–Fri, provides practical and emotional support for women with HIV and AIDS. **www.positivelywomen.org.uk**

Terrence Higgins Trust, 314–320 Gray's Inn Road, London WC1X 8DP, tel 020 7812 1600. Provides support and information for people affected with and by HIV and AIDS. For the THT Direct helpline, tel 0845 1221 200, Mon–Fri 10am–10pm, Sat–Sun 12 noon –6pm. See **www.tht.org.uk** for your nearest genito–urinary clinic. [Note: service for England and Wales but website contains useful information.]

Safety

PERSONAL SAFETY

Anti-Bullying Network, Network for teachers, parents and young people to share ideas how bullying in school and its consequences should be tackled. **www.antibullying.net**

Bullying Helpline, dedicated bullying helpline run by Childline Scotland, 0800 441111 is open 3.30–10pm on weekdays and 2–8pm Saturday and Sunday.

Commission for Racial Equality Scotland, The Tun, 12 Jacksons Entry, off Holyrood Road, Edinburgh, EH8 8PJ tel, 0131 524 2000, can give information on the law relating to racial harassment and the phone number of your local racial equality council. **www.cre.gov.uk**

Kidscape, 2 Grosvenor Gardens, London SW1W 0DH, tel 020 7730 3300 or 0845 1205 204, provides free information and advice on keeping safe, including bullying and how to cope with it, open Mon–Fri 10am–4pm. **www.kidscape.org.uk**

Rape Crisis Scotland, First Floor, Suite 58, Central Chambers, 93 Hope Street, Glasgow, G2 4LD, tel 0141 248 8848. Can give information on a nearest rape crisis or support service. **www.rapecrisisscotland.org.uk**

Survivors, 2 Leathermarket Street, London, SE1 3HN, email: info@survivorsuk.org.uk. A helpline, tel 0845 122 1201, is open Tues and Thurs 7–10pm, giving advice and information to men who are victims of sexual violence. **www.survivorsuk.co.uk**

Suzy Lamplugh Trust, National Centre for Personal Safety, Hampton House, 20 Albert Embankment, London SE1 7TJ, tel 020 7091 0014, email: trust@suzylamplugh.org. Practical information, guidance and resources on personal safety in all situations. **www.suzylamplugh.org**

VICTIMS AND COMPENSATION

Criminal Injuries Compensation Authority, Morley House, 26–30 Holborn Viaduct, London EC1A 2JQ, tel 020 7842 6800 and Tay House, 300 Bath Street, Glasgow, G2 4JN, tel 0141 331 2726, provides compensation for victims of crimes of violence. Information and application forms are available by post, telephone, tel 0800 358 3601 (Mon–Fri 9.00am–8.00pm, Sat 10.00am–6.00pm) or via the website, **www.cica.gov.uk**

Scottish Court Service, Hayweight House, 23 Lauriston Street, Edinburgh EH3 9DQ, tel 0131 229 9200 aims to help secure ready access to justice for the people of Scotland and can advise on court procedural and administrative matters **www.scotcourts.gov.uk**

Victim Support, 15/23 Hadwell Close, Edinburgh EH8 9RX, tel 0131 668 4486. There is a helpline providing support to people who have been victims of crime, Mon–Fri 9am–9pm and Sat–Sun 9am–7pm, tel 0845 30 30 900. **www.victimsupport.com**

Education

Education Law Unit – Govan Law Centre, 47 Burleigh Street, Glasgow G51 3LB, can respond to any queries about education laws in Scotland, tel 0141 445 1955, email advice@edlaw.org.uk. **www.edlaw.org.uk**

Learn Direct Scotland, offers information about places to study in Scotland, tel 0800 100 9000 (Mon–Fri 9am–9pm and Sat 9am –12 noon) **www.learndirectscotland.com**

Learning & Teaching Scotland, Gardyne Road, Dundee DD5 1NY, tel 01382 443 600 and 74 Victoria Crescent Road, Glasgow G12 9JN, tel 0141 337 5050.LT Scotland is a national public body which provides support, resources and staff development for early years and school education, and promotes learning throughout school life. **www.ltscotland.org.uk** Link through here to Parentzone website or go direct to **www.parentzonescotland.gov.uk**

Schoolhouse Home Education Association, PO Box 18044, Glenrothes, Fife KY7 9AD, provides information and advice for people choosing to educate their children out of school, tel 01307 463 120. **www.schoolhouse.org.uk**

Scottish Catholic Education Service, 75 Craigpark, Glasgow, G31 2HD, provides information on Scottish Catholic schools, tel 0141 556 4727, **www.sces.uk.com**

Scottish Council of Independent Schools, 21 Melville Street, Edinburgh EH3 7PE, tel 0131 220 2106, email: information@scis.org.uk for information on education in the independent sector **www.scis.org.uk**

Scottish Executive Education Department, Victoria Quay, Edinburgh EH6 6QQ, tel 0131 556 8400. **www.scotland.gov.uk** (navigate from Homepage to Education Department).

Scottish Qualifications Authority, Hanover House, 24 Douglas Street, Glasgow G2 7NQ and Ironmills Road, Dalkeith EH22 1LE. SQA is the national body responsible for the development, accreditation, assessment and certification of qualifications other than degrees. Customer contact number, tel 0845 279 1000. www.sqa.org.uk

Work and training

Careers Scotland, tel 08458 502502 for advice on careers.
www.careers-scotland.org.uk

Commission for Racial Equality Scotland, The Tun, 12 Jacksons Entry, off Holyrood Road, Edinburgh, EH8 8PJ, tel 0131 524 2000, email: scotland@cre.gov.uk. Information on all aspects of the Race Relations Acts, including problems with employment, housing, harassment and unfair discrimination. www.cre.gov.uk

Department for Education and Skills, Public Enquiry Unit, tel 0870 000 2288, for information on the law relating to both training and disabilities. www.dfes.gov.uk

Department of Trade and Industry, tel 020 7215 5000, for information on employment law. www.dti.gov.uk. For maternity pay www.tiger.gov.uk

Equal Opportunities Commission, St Stephen's House, 279 Bath Street, Glasgow G2 4JL, for information on a wide range of sex discrimination and gender issues. The Information Section is open Mon–Fri 9.30am–4.30pm. Helpline 08456 015901. www.eoc.org.uk

European Youth Portal, if you want to explore the possibility of going to another European country to study or work, or for voluntary work or exchanges, visit the European Youth Portal which was set up in May 2004: www.europa.eu/youth

Health and Safety Executive Information Services, Rose Court, 2 Southwark Bridge, London SE1 9HS. The Health & Safety Executive are responsible for checking health and safety at work. They can send information explaining the law and can tell you who to contact if you have a health and safety problem. They also run the HSE Infoline, tel 0845 345 0055, open Mon–Fri 8am–6pm. www.hse.gov.uk

The **National Minimum Wage Helpline** provides information about the National Minimum Wage, and can be used to make a complaint about an employer who is suspected of not paying the minimum wage, tel 0845 6000 678, open Mon–Fri 8.00am–6.00pm.

Stonewall Scotland, 9 Howe Street, Edinburgh, EH3 6TE, tel 0131 557 3679. Advising and campaigning on behalf of lesbians, gay men and bisexuals.
www.stonewallscotland.org.uk

Money

Association of British Insurers, Consumer Information Dept., 51 Gresham Street, London EC2V 7HQ, tel 020 7600 3333, for leaflets and further information on insurance.
www.abi.org.uk

Benefits, administered by the Department for Work and Pensions. For information on benefits, contact your local Jobcentre Plus or Social Security office listed in the phone book. The Disability and Carers service runs a free Benefit Enquiry Line for carers or people with an illness or disability, tel 0800 88 22 00.
www.dwp.gov.uk and
www.jobcentreplus.gov.uk

HM Revenue and Customs, for free information, leaflets and general enquiries contact any HMRC enquiry centre, see www.hmrc.gov.uk or your local phone box. For a self-assessment form, tel 0845 9000 404, 8am–10pm every day, including weekends and bank holidays. If you are not a taxpayer and want to claim back tax paid on deposits (bank, building society etc.), tel 0845 0776 543 during the same hours.

National Debtline, 0808 8084000 (free), for confidential help with debt problems and advice packs, email: advice@national debtline.co.uk www.nationaldebtline.co.uk

Office of Fair Trading, Fleetbank House, 2–6 Salisbury Square, London EC4Y 8JX. The official watchdog, protecting consumers' interests. They can't give advice on individual cases, but can send information on the law or put you in touch with someone who may be able to help. The Public Liaison Unit, tel 08457 22 44 99, can refer general enquiries and consumer complaints. www.oft.gov.uk

Trading Standards Offices, are in almost every town and city and give free advice on a wide range of consumer problems. The address of your local office will be in the phone book, under 'T', or available from your local council or from
www.tradingstandards.gov.uk

Family

Adoption Contact Register, the Contact Register has been founded by Missing Links UK for adopted people and their birth relatives, wishing contact with one another,

use the law with care **try talking first**

to be able to register their interest.
www.ukbirth-adoptionregister.com.

Birth Link, Family Care, 21 Castle Street, Edinburgh EH2 3DN.

British Association for Adoption and Fostering (BAAF), Saffron House, 6–10 Kirby Street, London EC1N 8TS, tel 020 7421 2600, provides advice and information for those thinking of adopting or fostering or tracing their birth parents. **www.BAAF.org.uk**.

Childline Scotland, free 24hr helpline for any child in danger and distress, tel 0800 1111. Freepost 1111, 18 Albion Street, Glasgow G1 1LH. **www.childline.org.uk**

Children 1st, 83 Whitehouse Loan, Edinburgh EH9 1AT, tel 0131 446 2300 (formerly Royal Scottish Society for Prevention of Cruelty to Children RSSPCC). **www.children1st.org.uk**

General Register Office for Scotland, New Register House, 3 West Register Street, Edinburgh, EH1 3YT for information on registration of births, marriages, deaths, divorces and adoptions in Scotland. **www.gro-scotland.gov.uk**

Kidscape, 2 Grosvenor Gardens, London SW1W 0DH, tel 020 7730 3300, provides free information and advice on keeping safe, including bullying and how to cope with it, open Mon–Fri 9am–4pm. **www.kidscape.org.uk**

Message Home Helpline, a confidential service allowing someone who has run away from home to leave a message for family and friends to let them know they are alive and well, **www.missingpersons.org**. If you are under 18, tel 0800 800 7070; over 18s, tel 0800 700740. Further information, including what to do if you want to talk to someone if you are thinking about leaving home or wish to return home, can be found at **www.runawayhelpline.org**.

NORCAP, 112 Church Road, Wheatley, Oxfordshire OX33 1LU, tel 01865 875 000, provides advice and support for adopted people and their birth relatives who wish to get in touch. Open Mon, 10am–12noon, 1–4pm, 5–7.30pm, Tues–Fri, 10am–12.30pm, 1pm–4.30pm **www.norcap.org.uk**

One-Parent Families Scotland, offers a helpline on 0800 018 5026 for lone parents, pregnant women on topics such as benefits, employment, maintenance, childcare and parenting problems. OPFS, 13 Gayfield Square, Edinburgh EH1 3NX, tel 0131 556 3899, email: info@opfs.org.uk **www.opfs.org.uk**

Parentline Plus, 520 Highgate Studios, 53–79 Highgate Road, Kentish Town, London NW5 1TL, tel (free) 0808 800 2222, works with adults, children and young people providing information and support to families. **www.parentlineplus.org.uk**

Runaway provides a free helpline, tel 0808 800 7070, for young people under 18 who have run away or been forced to leave home or care. Can give confidential advice, make referrals and arrange help.

Scottish Child Law Centre, 1st Floor, Old College, South Bridge, Edinburgh EH8 9YL. Offers advice on a wide range of issues by letter and phone. The advice line is open Mon–Wed and Fri 9.30am–4pm; Thur 6–7.30pm. Tel 0800 328 8970.

Scottish Women's Aid gives information, support and advice for women experiencing domestic violence in the home. Groups all over Scotland, and you can phone up or visit them during office hours. Also available Scottish Domestic Abuse Helpline 0800 027 1234, available 10am–12pm, 7days. **www.scottishwomensaid.co.uk**

Home

Crisis, 64 Commercial Street, London E1 1LT, tel 0870 011 33 55, email: enquiries@crisis.org.uk gives advice and assistance to homeless people. **www.crisis.org.uk**

The Foyer Federation, 5–9 Hatton Wall, London EC!N 8HX tel 020 7430 2212, a UK wide youth homeless charity providing accommodation, education and training opportunities for 16–25 year olds with housing needs. For details of the nearest Foyer see **www.foyer.net**

Shelter Scotland, 4th Floor, Scotia Bank House, 6 South Charlotte Street, Edinburgh EH2 4AW, campaigns to improve the housing conditions and rights of private tenants. Shelter also has a network of housing aid centres across the country and runs Shelterline, a free 24hr national housing helpline tel 0808 800 4444. **www.shelterscotland.org.uk**

Leisure

Citizencard, PO Box 1221, Newcastle-under-Lyme ST5 0US, provide free photo-ID card and proof of age for under 18s and charge £7 for over 18s, tel, 0870 240 1221. **www.citizencard.net**

Proof of Age Card Scheme, The Portman Group, 7–10 Chandos Street, Cavendish Square, London W1G 9DQ, tel 020 7907 3700. If you're 18 or over you can get a Proof of Age Card from the Portman Group for £5, call 01782 741 968, email: info@portmangroup.org.uk, **www.portman-group.org.uk**

Royal Society for Protection of Birds (RSPB), for advice on protected birds see **www.rspb.org.uk**

Scottish Environment Protection Agency (SEPA), has a 24hr emergency pollution hotline 0800 807060. For general enquiries contact SEPA Corporate Office, Erskine Court, Castle Business Park, STIRLING FK9 4TR, tel: 01786 457700. **www.sepa.org.uk**

Scottish Natural Heritage, 12 Hope Terrace, Edinburgh EH9 2AS, tel 0131 447 4784, for information on of access to land and inland water for outdoor recreation, www.snh.org.uk Also, for information on Scottish Rights of Way, see **www.scotways.com**

Scottish Society for the Prevention of Cruelty to Animals (Scottish SPCA), have hotline numbers to report an animal in distress: Inverness and Highland, tel 01463 231 191, Aberdeen, tel 01224 581 236, South and Central Belt, tel 0870 73 77722. For all other queries contact Braehead Mains, 603 Queensferry Road, Edinburgh EH4 6EA tel 0131 339 0222 **www.scottishspca.org**

Young Scot PASS card – this is usually issued through your local authority and you are advised to speak to your school administrator to find out how to get one.

Travel and transport

ABTA (The Association of British Travel Agents), 68–71 Newman Street, London W1T 3AH, for information and advice over problems with a package holiday, tel 020 7637 2444, **www.abta.com**

Department of Health, health-related travel advice and online EHIC applications, tel 020 7210 4850 (Mon–Fri 9am–5pm). **www.dh.gov.uk/travellers**

Department of Transport, for information on motoring and transport law. **www.dft.gov.uk**. Enquiries, tel 020 7944 8300. For public transport information, tel 0870 608 2608.

Driving Standards Agency, Stanley House, 56 Talbot Street, Nottingham NG1 5GU, tel 0115 901 2500 for information on driving tests for cars and compulsory basic training for motorcyclists. **www.driving-tests.co.uk**

DVLA, Licensing Centre, Longview Road, Swansea SA6 7JL, for enquiries about driving licences, tax discs or the registration details of a particular vehicle. Driver enquiries, tel 0870 240 0009; vehicle enquiries, tel 0870 240 0010. **www.dvla.gov.uk**

Euro<26 Card, see National Youth Agency site at **www.nya.org.uk/euro26**

National Express Ltd., Ensign Court, 4 Vicarage Road, Edgbaston, Birmingham B15 3ES. Information on coach travel and discount travel schemes. For telephone bookings call 0870 5 80 80 80, open every day 8am–8pm. **www.nationalexpress.com**. For the disabled persons travel helpline, tel 0121 423 8479.

Royal Society for the Prevention of Accidents (RoSPA), Slateford House, Lanark Road, Edinburgh EH14 1TL, tel 0131 444 1155, email: help@rospa.com. Information on safety on the road and in the home. For a quicker reply, enclose a SAE. **www.rospa.com**

Young Persons Railcard, ATOC Ltd, 3rd Floor, 40 Bernard St., London WC1N 1BY. **www.youngpersons-railcard.co.uk**

Police and courts

Citizens' Advice Bureau (CAB), have trained staff who can give free legal advice and suggest solicitors able to deal with your particular problem. See General section, for contact details.

Complaints Against the Police. Anyone who wishes to make a complaint about the police should do so first to the force concerned. If, once the complaint has been investigated and concluded, the person making the complaint is not satisfied about the way the complaint was handled, they may write to HM Chief Inspector of Constabulary, First Floor West, St Andrew's House, Regent Road, Edinburgh EH1 3DG, tel 0131 244 5614, email: HMIC2@scotland.gsi.gov.uk

Scottish Court Service, Hayweight House, 23 Lauriston Street, Edinburgh EH3 9DQ, tel 0131 229 9200 provides information relating to all civil and criminal courts within Scotland and publishes information on what you can expect if you are charged with a criminal offence or attend court as a witness, member of a jury or as a defendant or plaintiff in a civil case, email: enquiries@scotcourts.gov.uk, **www.scotcourts.gov.uk**

use the law with care **try talking first**

CONTACTS

Scottish Legal Aid Board, 44 Drumsheugh Gardens, Edinburgh EH3 7SW, tel 0131 226 7061, email: general@slab.org.uk. Legal aid allows people who would not otherwise be able to afford it to get help for their legal problems. There is a Legal Aid Helpline, tel 0845 122 8686 (Open 7 Days a week 7am–11pm). **www.slab.org.uk**

Law, government and human rights

POLITICAL PARTIES

Scottish Conservatives, 83 Princes Street, Edinburgh EH2 2ER, tel 0131 247 6890. **www.scottishconservatives.com**

Scottish Green Party, 3 Lyne Street, Edinburgh EH7 5DN, tel 08700 772 207. **www.scottishgreens.org.uk**

Scottish Labour Party, John Smith House, 145 West Regent Street, Glasgow G2 4RE, tel 0141 572 6900. **www.scottishlabour.org.uk**

Scottish Liberal Democrats, 4 Clifton Terrace, Edinburgh EH12 5DR, tel 0131 337 2314 **www.scotlibdems.org.uk**

Scottish National Party, 107 McDonald Road, Edinburgh EH7 4NW, tel 0131 525 8900. **www.snp.org**

Scottish Socialist Party, (Glasgow office) 70 Stanley Street, Glasgow G41 1JB, tel 0141 429 8200; (Edinburgh office) 17–23 Calton Road, Edinburgh EH8 6DG, tel 0131 557 0426. **www.scottishsocialistparty.org**

Solidarity, PO Box 7565, Glasgow, G42 2DN. **www.solidarityscotland.org**

GENERAL

House of Commons Information Office, House of Commons, London SW1A 0AA, tel 020 7219 3000. A public information service on the working and proceedings of Parliament. **www.parliament.uk**

Human Rights Scotland, 204–206 Baltic Chambers, 50 Wellington Street, Glasgow G2 6HJ, tel 0141 229 1140, have publications on the Human Rights Act. **www.scotrights.org.uk**

For information on the **Human Rights Act**, refer to the Department for Constitutional Affairs website **www.dca.gov.uk/hract**

Scottish Parliament, Edinburgh EH99 1SP, tel 0131 348 5000/0845 278 1999 **www.scottish.parliament.uk**

Scottish Youth Parliament aim to be the collective national youth voice for all young people in Scotland aged between 14 and 25 years. **www.scottishyouthparliament.org.uk**

The Scottish Information Commissioner, Kinburn Castle, Doubledykes Road, St Andrews, Fife KY16 9DS, tel 01334 464 610, have responsibility for overseeing the workings of the Freedom of Information (Scotland) Act 2002. **www.itspublicknowledge.info**

The Information Commissioner's Office, Wycliffe House, Water Lane, Wilmslow, Cheshire SK9 5AF has responsibility for overseeing the workings of the Data Protection Act 1998 and the Freedom of Information Act 2000. A helpline is open during normal office hours, tel 01625 545 745. **www.informationcommissioner.gov.uk**

The European Union

The Council of Europe, an organisation with a strong interest in human rights, which works to find solutions to some of the problems facing European society, Avenue de L'Europe, 67075 Strasbourg Cedex, France, tel +33(0)3 88 41 20 33, email: infopoint@coe.int; **www.coe.int**

European Commission, can indicate your nearest centre for information, tel 020 7973 1992. Representation in the UK, 8 Storey's Gate, London, SW1P 3AT, tel 020 7973 1900. **www.cec.org.uk**

European Parliament Information Office, 2 Queen Anne's Gate, London SW1H 9AA, tel 020 7227 4300. For a free information service on the European Parliament, where you will be given contact details for your specific enquiry, tel 00 800 678 91011 (free, 8.00am–5.30pm UK time). **www.europarl.org.uk**

European Youth Forum (EYF), Rue Josephllstraat 120, B–1000 Brussels, tel +32 2 230 64 90, represents youth organisations from all over Europe and serves to channel the flow of information and opinions between young people and decision-makers. For more information on how to become involved, **www.youthforum.org**.

Organising Bureau of School Students Unions, Rue de la Sablonniere 20, Brussels, tel +32(0) 264 72 390. OBESSU coordinates national organisations of school students. **www.obessu.org**.

A

Abortion 16
Abusive phone calls 24
Accommodation
- agencies 76
- deposits 77
- eviction 80-81
- finding 76
- lodgings 79
- rent 76-80
- repairs 80
- service charge 77
- tenancy agreement 78-80
Adoption 15, 69
Age
- of consent 13-14
- of criminal responsibility 117
- proof of 85
AIDS 11, 17-18
Alcohol 21, 84-86, 89, 91, 105
Animals 94
Apprenticeships 35-38
Assault 20-22, 87
- indecent 13, 23-24
- in marriage 71

B

Baby-sitting 69
Bail 113
Banks 56, 97
Beaches 93
Bigamy 71
Blood donors 8
Bulls 92
Burglary 21
Bus travel 98-99

C

Charters
- Passengers' 99
- Redundancy Payments Service 49
- Victim's 20
Cheque guarantee card 56
Children's Panel 116
Citizen's arrest 20
Citizenship 67
Coach travel 99
Consumer law 52, 55, 58, 60, 84-85, 96, 103

Contraception 14
Contract
- consumer 52-55, 84, 85, 96, 99
- employment 36, 39-40, 47-48
Copyright 90
Corporal punishment 29, 68, 122
Courts 116-118
- district 116
- high 117
- Scottish Court Service 20, 118
- sheriff 117
- small claims 55
- youth 116
Crash helmets 104
Credit 58-60
Credit cards 58-59, 96
Crime, reporting to the police 20
Criminal Injuries Compensation Authority 20, 23
Crown Office 116
Customs 98
Cycling 102

D

Debt 61
Dentists 7
Discrimination
- at work 18, 37, 45-47,
- disability 45, 88
- housing 76
- race 45, 77, 84, 124, 135
- sex 45-47, 85, 87, 124
Divorce 71-73
Doctors
- confidentiality 6, 14
- registering and changing 6
Drugs
- illegal 10-12, 86, 89
- police powers 12
Duty solicitor 111, 118

E

Elections 126-128
Electoral register 126
Employment tribunal 37, 41-43, 50

Engagements 71
Euro 135
European Convention on Human Rights 122-127
European Council 136
European Parliament 128, 137
European Union 121, 132-139
Eviction 80-81

F

Fingerprints 112
Fishing 93
Footpaths 92

G

Gambling 87
Gay relationships 14, 45
Glue sniffing 12
Grandparents 74

H

Harassment 22-23
- by landlord 81-82
- racial 22-23
- sexual 46
Hire purchase 60
HIV 17-18
Holidays 96-99
Homelessness 82
Housing benefit 76
Human rights 122-125

I

Industrial action 48
Insurance 62-63
- household 81, 89
- motor vehicle 88, 98, 101, 106
- travel 96-97

J

Judicial review 132
Juries 117-118

K

Knives 21

INDEX

L

Leaving home 68, 77
Legal advice
- at the police station 111
- in court 116
Legal Aid 118
Living together 70
Loans 60

M

Marriage 67, 70-71
Medical treatment
- complaints 8
- consent to 6, 8, 14, 69
- records 9
Mental health 126
MEPs 127-129, 139
Motor cycles 98, 100-101
Motor vehicles
- accidents 106
- buying a car 103
- drinking & driving 105
- insurance 88, 98, 101, 106
- learning to drive 100
- licence 100, 105
- MOT 101
- offences 101-102, 104-106
- on holiday 98
- seat belts 104
- speeding 104
- stolen 104
- tax disc 99
MPs 120, 127-129

N

Names 66
Neighbours 81, 90
Nightclubs 87
Noise 81, 86, 90

O

Offensive weapons 21
Ombudsman 126
Opticians 8

P

Parental responsibility 66, 68-70, 73
Parents and children 66-70, 72-73

Parliament 120
Passports 96-97
Pets 94
Police
- arrest 112-115
- caution 111
- codes of practice 108
- complaints against the 113
- powers 11, 85-86, 102, 104, 108-113
- questioning 111-113
- search 9, 109-110
Pollution 93
Pregnancy 15
Prescriptions 6
Procurator Fiscal 114
Prostitution 18
Protest 130-131

R

Rail travel 98-99
Rape 23, 121
Raves 86
Religion, choosing your 69, 124
Restaurants 84-85
Rivers 93
Robbery 21

S

School
- attendance, 26, 28, 68
- bullying 32
- charges 27
- choice of 26
- drugs in 11, 30
- exams 32
- exclusion 31
- leaving age 27
- records 31
- religious education 28
- rules 28-30
- sex education 28
- uniform 29
Scottish Parliament 120-121
Self-defence 21
Service charges 77
Sex
- consent to 13, 23
- under age 13-14
- unlawful 14

Sexually transmitted infection 17
Solvent abuse 12
Sport 91
Squatting 82
Step-parents 73

T

Tattoos 8
Tax 64
Taxis 88
Television licence 90
Tenancy agreement 78-80
Theft 21
Tobacco 12
Trade unions 48
Training 35-38
Trespass 89, 92, 132

V

Victims of crime 21-23
Violence, in the home 71
Voting 127-128, 137

W

Wills 8, 70
Witnesses 20
Work
- abroad 137
- applying for 38-39
- contract 36, 39-41, 45, 47
- discrimination 37, 43-46, 140
- dismissal 49-50
- drugs at 11
- health and safety 37, 43-44
- HIV & AIDS 11
- holidays 43
- hours 34, 36, 43
- maternity rights 47
- part-time 34-35, 40, 47, 140
- pay 41
- redundancy 49-50, 141
- young people 34